For my grandchildren

Robert, Mary, Emma and Jacob

For UK order enquiries: please contact Bookpoint Ltd,
130 Milton Park, Abingdon, Oxon OX14 4SB.
Telephone: +44 (0) 1235 827720. *Fax:* +44 (0) 1235 400454.
Lines are open 09.00–17.00, Monday to Saturday, with a 24-hour
message answering service. Details about our titles and how to
order are available at www.hoddereducation.com

British Library Cataloguing in Publication Data: a catalogue record for this title
is available from the British Library.

First published in UK 2011 by Hodder Education, part of Hachette UK,
338 Euston Road, London NW1 3BH.

Typeset by MPS Limited, a Macmillan Company.

Printed in Great Britain for Hodder Education, an Hachette UK Company,
338 Euston Road, London NW1 3BH, by CPI Cox & Wyman, Reading,
Berkshire RG1 8EX.

The publisher has used its best endeavours to ensure that the URLs for
external websites referred to in this book are correct and active at the time of
going to press. However, the publisher and the author have no responsibility
for the websites and can make no guarantee that a site will remain live or
that the content will remain relevant, decent or appropriate.

Hachette UK's policy is to use papers that are natural, renewable and
recyclable products and made from wood grown in sustainable forests.
The logging and manufacturing processes are expected to conform to the
environmental regulations of the country of origin.

Impression number   10 9 8 7 6 5 4 3 2 1
Year   2015 2014 2013 2012 2011

THANK YOUS

I'm tremendously grateful to Lesley Staff and Carrie Geddes for their sensitive
advice and encouragement, as well as their editorial skills.

I'm also grateful to a wide range of people who have generously commended
the longer book on which this Flash edition is based, including Archbishop
Rowan Williams ('An exciting and engaging book') and Archbishop Sentamu
('Well-researched, accessible ... invaluable').

John Young, York

Contents

Meet the author – John Young

I've had a variety of jobs – paperboy, postman, hospital porter, farmhand, soldier (National Service), teacher, lecturer, occasional broadcaster and journalist, author, Anglican Minister. My early ambition to be a professional footballer remains unfulfilled thus far ...

I have a love-hate relationship with writing (it's hard work!) but to my surprise I've written more than 30 books/booklets and around half a million copies of these are in circulation. My work has been translated into several languages, including Chinese and Russian.

I worked for two Archbishops of York, and was a member of the General Synod of the Church of England for many years. Today I'm a Canon Emeritus of York Minster. I've preached in some of Britain's great cathedrals – including St Paul's, where the entire back row got up and walked out. (I like to think they were tourists who had a bus to catch, but ...)

It's been a huge privilege to broadcast occasionally on BBC Radio 2, Radio 4 and the World Service. A personal highlight came when Radio 4 selected for its *Pick of the Week* a modern 'parable' which I'd written and presented.

Arising from my work as a broadcaster and co-founder of York Courses, I've interviewed a number of eminent Christians including the Archbishop of Canterbury, Professor Sir John Houghton (climatologist) and Revd Dr John Polkinghorne (former Professor of Mathematical Physics at Cambridge University). These conversations are available on CD from www.yorkcourses.co.uk

Introduction

Christianity is the world religion which is based on the life and ministry of Jesus, who is also called Jesus Christ ('Christ' means *Messiah*).

At the heart of Christianity there is a profound puzzle. For this huge and influential movement is based upon an apparent failure.

Jesus died young. He suffered a terrible, shameful death. He left no writings. The only record of his life and teaching was in the memories of his followers. When the pressure was on, they drifted away. One betrayed him; another denied all knowledge of him.

The movement he founded had never been very large, even after three years in the public eye. By the time of his death it had crumbled to nothing – apart from a few demoralized, frightened friends. It looked like just one more heroic – but futile – attempt to stand against authority.

Yet the stubborn fact remains. From that hopeless beginning, the movement grew. And grew. And grew. It became the largest, most influential movement of all time. The world dates its calendar from its Founder's birth.

These are facts that cry out for adequate explanation. The explanation given in the Bible is the only one that gets near to solving this immense puzzle. Three days after Roman soldiers nailed Jesus to the cross, God raised him from the dead. Jesus defeated death. This glorious event has huge implications for all of us. It is celebrated at Easter – the Church's greatest festival. A few weeks later (at Pentecost) God sent the Holy Spirit – the Spirit of Jesus himself – into the hearts and lives of his followers.

No longer afraid and dismayed, they told the world about God's love revealed in Jesus. The long – and fascinating – story of Christianity had begun ...

1

the central figure

Albert Einstein is famous for writing just three letters: $E = mc^2$

Less well known are his following words:
'I am a Jew, but I am enthralled by the luminous figure of the Nazarene ... No one can read the Gospels without feeling the actual presence of Jesus. His personality pulsates in every word. No myth is filled with such life.'

Einstein stands in a long line of people who bear witness to the greatness of Jesus. The influential Hindu pacifist Mahatma Gandhi is another, as is US president Barack Obama.

Jesus of Nazareth is a figure in history. But his immense impact continues to be felt by millions in the twenty-first century.

The impact of Jesus

Professor Hans Küng, a leading Christian scholar, makes the following points about Jesus Christ and the faith which bears his name:

> **None of the great founders of religions lived in so restricted an area. None lived for such a terribly short time. None died so young. And yet how great his influence has been ... Numerically, Christianity is well ahead of all world religions.**

> (*On Being a Christian*, Collins)

This is not quoted in a spirit of competitive superiority; it is nothing more nor less than a statement of significant fact. In considering the Christian faith, we are studying the largest movement in history. Christianity has exercised tremendous influence (for good and ill) upon our world.

Jesus has been the focus of more study, more controversy and more art than any other figure. He is the one who has 'chopped history in half': BC *before Christ*; AD *Anno Domini* – in the year of Our Lord (sometimes called CE or *Common Era*). In today's world, millions of people – from every continent and nearly every country – claim some allegiance to him. Christians make up about one-third of the world's population.

Ralph Waldo Emerson, the American essayist, summed up the significance of Jesus when he said that his impact is not so much *written on*, as *ploughed into*, the history of the world. All this is remarkable enough. But when we consider the short and rather obscure life of Jesus, it becomes extraordinary.

The teaching of Jesus

Christianity is based not only on ideas, but on events. At its centre we do not find a theory, but a person: Jesus Christ. Many people have a sentimental picture of Jesus. They view him as a rather anaemic character, more interested in flowers, birds and

children than in the harsh world of adult reality. How different is
the towering figure of the New Testament. We see there:

* a man marked out as a dangerous rebel by the authorities
* a man who drew large crowds
* a man who inspired others
* a man who took the uncompromising road to martyrdom
* a man of deep passion and decisive action.

The Gospels assure us that Jesus *was* interested in children and
in nature. And with the down-trodden he was very gentle. But the
world he inhabited was a harsh world of hatred, intrigue, brutality and
revenge. The Gospels portray a dynamic figure who waged war against
evil with the weapons of love, openness, honesty and forgiveness.
His honesty was fearless. Against those greatest sins of pride,
hypocrisy and indifference, his attack was blistering and devastating.

Jesus did not set out to be an 'original' teacher. As a Jew he
stood in a tradition which was steeped in the Hebrew Scriptures
(known to Christians as the Old Testament). He drew on those
Scriptures, and his central demands – that we should love God with
all our heart and our neighbour as ourselves – link two separate Old
Testament texts (Deuteronomy 6:5; Leviticus 19:18). This was his
genius: to make new connections, to bring fresh emphases, to take
old ideas and give them new content, to reveal the deeper meaning
which was latent within them.

The Kingdom of God

Jesus spoke frequently about 'the Kingdom of God' or
'the Kingdom of heaven'. This idea is certainly found in the Jewish
Scriptures. But Jesus put it at the *centre* of his teaching and
illustrated (but never defined) its meaning with a series of brilliant,
yet often puzzling, pictures and parables. In this way he made his
hearers, and now his readers, think very hard.

> *The kingdom of heaven is like treasure hidden in a field.*
> *When a man found it, he hid it again, and then in his joy went*
> *and sold all he had and bought that field. Again, the kingdom*

of heaven is like a merchant looking for fine pearls. When he found one of great value, he went away and sold everything he had and bought it.

(Matthew 13:44–46)

Jesus made it clear that his notion of God's kingly rule was very different from the popular views of his time. His country was under enemy occupation. The hated Romans were in charge and there were many Jews who looked for armed revolt. Their nation had a famous history of success on the battlefield; perhaps this teacher would be the new military leader? To those who wanted to go down that road, Jesus was a great disappointment: 'My kingdom is not of this world' (John 18:36). In *his* Kingdom, disciples would turn the other cheek and leadership must be characterized by humble service.

Miracles of the kingdom

Many miracles are recorded in the Gospels, demonstrating Jesus' power over sickness, sin, nature, demons and death. When his enemies accused him of healing by Satan's power he replied, 'But if I drive out demons by the finger of God, then the kingdom of God has come to you' (Luke 11:20).

God's kingly rule was present because Jesus was present. But his ministry was also the sign of a future in which God's kingly rule would be fulfilled and consummated. One day the 'Son of Man' will come 'in his Father's glory with the holy angels' (Mark 8:38). *Now* and *not yet* are held in balance.

Parables of the kingdom

Jesus became famous for his stories or parables. A parable is a story which works on two levels. It is 'an earthly story with a heavenly meaning'. At one level it is an interesting tale with strong human interest. But the story has a deeper meaning and a personal application. Jesus' hearers are usually left to work this out for themselves. Some parables convey the notion of *growth*. Others convey a sense of *crisis*: decisions must be made, sides must be taken. Jesus' stories are usually about people.

The best known parables are The Good Samaritan and The Prodigal Son. The former is not just an exhortation to compassion and kindness (though it is that). It is a strong attack upon racism and bigotry. Samaritans were widely despised by Jews and vice versa. Jesus was taking a huge risk in making a *Samaritan* the hero, in contrast to the establishment figures of his own race and religion. Here were the seeds of conflict with the authorities which would end in his death by crucifixion.

> *The teaching of Jesus stands on an Everest alone. No other teaching has had the same impact and influence, in countless lives and diverse cultures. No other teaching has provoked so much change, or stirred so much debate.*
>
> (Professor Sir Norman Anderson)
>
> Alec McCowen, the British actor, set out to memorize St Mark's account of the ministry and death of Jesus – as a hobby! To his surprise, large audiences around the world wanted to hear his recitation of the life of Jesus, taken straight from the Bible. When asked what he made of the story he replied: 'Something absolutely marvellous happened in Palestine 2000 years ago.'

The anguish of the Prodigal Son is captured powerfully by the sculptor Rodin, whose bronze figure of the Prodigal is in the Tate Collection. Archbishop Desmond Tutu describes the significance of this story with typical vigour and enthusiasm:

> *What a tremendous relief ... to discover that we don't need to prove ourselves to God. That is what Jesus came to say, and for that he got killed ... The Good News is that God loves me long before I could have done anything to deserve it. He is like the father of the prodigal son, waiting anxiously for the return of his wayward son ... That is tremendous stuff – that is the Good News.*

The parable of the Prodigal Son could equally well be entitled *The Forgiving Father*. Again, the notion of God as Father was familiar to Jesus' contemporaries. But Jesus underlined its importance, stressing both the *rule* and the *love* of God.

He emphasized his own close relationship with God and taught that discipleship cannot be reduced to a set of rules. At its heart is a relationship with the living God, who is 'your Heavenly Father' – to be loved and trusted. But a loving father is not a doting uncle.

Much of Jesus' teaching is uncompromising in its moral and spiritual demands:

* turn the other cheek (Matthew 5:39)
* go the extra mile (Matthew 5:41)
* judge not or you will be judged (Matthew 7:1)
* forgive seventy times seven (Matthew 18:22)
* sell your possessions and give to the poor (Mark 10:21).

His teaching makes intellectual demands too. Jesus did not spoonfeed his largely uneducated audience; he respected their intelligence. He often said things that he did not mean! By exaggeration and paradox Jesus left, and leaves, his hearers thinking furiously, 'He can't really mean *that*. So just what does he mean ...':

* let the dead bury their dead (Matthew 8:22)
* become like a little child (Matthew 18:3)
* cut off a foot rather than allow it to lead to sin (Mark 9:45)
* hate your father and mother (Luke 14:26)
* you must be born again (John 3:3).

A father's love includes discipline as well as encouragement. Hence Jesus taught us to *trust* God, to *love* God and to *fear* God – to hold him in respect and awe, for God *is* GOD. He emphasized that prayer, forgiveness, honesty, humility and generosity are all involved in accepting God's kingly rule in our lives. All this is summed up in the world's most famous prayer, given by Jesus in response to his disciples' request, 'Lord teach us to pray':

> *Father, hallowed be your name, your kingdom come.*
> *Give us each day our daily bread.*
> *Forgive us our sins, for we also forgive everyone who sins against us.*
> *And lead us not into temptation.*

(Luke 11:2; see Matthew 6:9–13)

A puzzle

Jesus taught humility. He associated with and served ordinary people. He chose fishermen for his close companions. He lived a simple, rough life, and befriended outcasts such as prostitutes and tax-collectors who collaborated with the hated Romans. Yet in an unassuming way, he made explosive claims. The New Testament scholar Bishop John Robinson summed up:

> *He steps in the eyes of his contemporaries into the space reserved for God ... It is impossible to escape the conclusion that he went around not just talking about God (that would not have provoked the reaction he did) but standing in God's place, acting and speaking for him.*

> (*Can We Trust the New Testament?*, Mowbray)

Jesus: more than a man?

All the New Testament writers assert the human nature of Jesus. Like us he got hungry, thirsty and tired. He experienced the full range of human emotions, including joy, sorrow and desolation. But in a remarkably short space of time, the early Christians came to the startling conclusion that Jesus was *divine* as well as human. This resulted partly from their belief in his resurrection. But their conclusion finds its seeds in the teaching of Jesus himself. Jesus did not go around saying, 'I am God.' Indeed, he joyfully acknowledged his dependence upon God his 'heavenly Father'. He was no usurper. *But he did claim a unique relationship with God; he did claim a unique mission from God; and he did claim that he, and only he, was able to do things which it was proper only for God to do*.

In this way Jesus himself laid the foundations for the kind of language used about him in the New Testament and (later) in the Nicene and other Creeds. As the New Testament scholar Professor C H Dodd put it: '*His words carried divine authority and his actions were instinctive with divine power.*' Over the years the distinctive Christian view of God emerged. He is three 'Persons' in one God: Father, Son and Holy Spirit. This doctrine of the Trinity was not invented by the early Christians; it has its seeds in the teaching of

Jesus himself. Those seeds can be seen in bloom on other pages in the New Testament.

> * *He is the image of the invisible God, the firstborn over all creation ... all things were created by him and for him.*
>
> (Colossians 1:15–16)

> * *Your attitude should be the same as that of Christ Jesus:*
>   *Who, being in very nature God,*
>   *did not consider equality with God*
>   *something to be grasped ...*
>
> (Philippians 2:5, 6)

> * *Thomas said to him [Jesus], 'My Lord and my God!'*
>
> (John 20:28)

At the same time, the New Testament writers held that Jesus *was a real human being*. Their concern was to declare that God reveals himself through Jesus Christ – not to speculate on the innermost nature of God. Such speculation came later, as Christians pondered the relationship between Father, Son and Holy Spirit. The result of this mature consideration can be seen in the Nicene and other Creeds.

'Who do you say that I am?' (Mark 8:29)

Any study of Christianity is bound to focus on Jesus Christ. And any study of Jesus leaves each of us with a personal challenge. It is impossible to understand Christianity from a Christian perspective, without experiencing this challenge.

Jesus continues to issue his gentle invitation, which is also a tough command: 'Come, follow me.' Michael Ramsey, 100th Archbishop of Canterbury, expressed this challenge with powerful simplicity as he described some of the claims of Christ which we have considered, and drew out their implications.

> *Perhaps you are trying the line that you welcome Christ's moral teaching and admire it: but reject his own claims. It seems to me a most unconvincing line. The moral teaching and the claims are woven in one, for both concern the reign of God.*

I see no escape from the dilemma: either Jesus is fraudulent, or his claim is true: either we judge him for being terribly amiss, or we let him judge us. That was, in fact, the dilemma that cut through the consciences of his contemporaries.

(*Introducing the Christian Faith*, SCM Press)

Conclusion: Jesus our contemporary

This then is the Jesus of the New Testament, the Jesus of history and the Jesus for today – whenever *our* 'today' might be. He comes to us with tough demands – calling us to serve a troubled and divided world in his name and with his strength. He comes, too, with unutterable comfort.

To a world beset by problems he comes as guide. In a world where many are lonely, he comes as friend. To a world which often seems to lack meaning, he brings understanding. For a world tempted to despair, he provides the ground for hope. Over a world where dying is the single certainty, he sits enthroned as the conqueror of death.

The words of Jesus as recorded in St John's Gospel have been tested and proved in countless lives: '*I am the light of the world. Whoever follows me will never walk in darkness, but will have the light of life*' (John 8:12).

With the help of the Dead Sea Scrolls and Jewish literature, in particular the major work of the Jewish historian Fabius Josephus, you can reconstruct Jewish life of that age, and you put Jesus into this, and he emerges as a living figure, not someone who fell down from heaven.

(Professor Geza Vermes, Jewish Biblical scholar)

On a spring morning in about the year 30 CE three men were executed by the Roman authorities in Judaea. Two were 'brigands' ... the third was convicted of having claimed to be 'King of the Jews' – a political title. It turned out that the third man, Jesus of Nazareth, would become one of the most important figures in human history.

(E P Sanders in *The Historical Figure of Jesus*, Penguin)

2

crucified Saviour

When considering Jesus' death, Christianity focuses on two central ideas:

* First: Jesus suffered *for* us
* Second: even now, Jesus suffers *with* us.

My God, my God, why have you forsaken me? Perhaps surprisingly, these bleak words of Jesus from the cross brought comfort to a bereaved mother. 'You see', she said, 'Jesus knows just how I feel.' Jesus' cry of dereliction was for her an affirmation – not a denial – of faith in God.

Archbishop Desmond Tutu expressed his infectious faith in the centrality of the cross of Christ with typical gusto – demonstrating that Christianity is not fixated on death, but on LIFE:

What a tremendous relief ... to discover that we don't need to prove ourselves to God. That is what Jesus came to say, and for that he got killed ... That is tremendous stuff – that is the Good News. Whilst we were yet sinners, says St Paul, Christ died for us. God did not wait until we were die-able for, for He could have waited until the cows came home.

The cross has become *the* central symbol of Christianity. Not only do we find a cross or crucifix within most churches, but many church buildings are designed in cruciform shape. The two great sacraments of the Church focus on the cross. *Baptism* is 'into Christ', and especially into his death and resurrection. In *Holy Communion*, the bread and wine refer to the broken body and shed blood of Jesus.

* * *

Towards the end of his three years in the public eye, Jesus faced a crucial decision. Should he return home to the safety of Galilee? Or should he go on to Jerusalem and to conflict? In his Gospel, Luke tells us that 'Jesus resolutely set out for Jerusalem.' That decision led to his death.

In Mark's Gospel we find a refrain on Jesus' lips: 'The Son of Man must suffer.' And in John's Gospel, Jesus refers to his death as his 'hour'. Everything he taught and did led up to his climactic death. This is seen most clearly in the dramatic events of the last week of his life.

The week began with his entry into Jerusalem. Jesus timed this to coincide with the great Jewish festival of Passover, when Jerusalem was teeming with pilgrims. His reputation ensured a large crowd. He rode on a humble donkey, fulfilling the prophecy of Zechariah 9:9.

Here was no worldly king, coming in glittering style to impress and command. Here was the Prince of Peace, riding in great humility. The crowds greeted him with shouts: 'Hosanna', which means '*Save Now*'. They scattered coats and palm branches on the road (hence *Palm Sunday*). As he approached Jerusalem, Jesus wept bitterly over the city. For some days, he taught in the precincts of the Temple – a fabulous building erected by King Herod 'the Great', who had tried to kill him as a baby. Jesus made a direct attack on the attitudes and practices of many of the leaders of his people. He even drove out those who were trading in the Temple precincts. '*It is written*', he said to them, '*My house shall be a house of prayer, but you have made it a den of robbers*' (Luke 19:46).

> *The central Christian belief is that Christ's death has somehow put us right with God and given us a fresh start. Theories as to how it did this are another matter. A good many different theories have been held as to how it works; what all Christians are agreed on is that it does work.*
>
> (C S Lewis)

To mark the annual Passover festival, Jewish people gathered in their homes to eat a celebration supper – a practice which continues to this day. This was the last supper which Jesus ate with his disciples; it was to become the most celebrated meal in history. After they had eaten, Judas – one of the 12 disciples – left the room and betrayed Jesus to the Jewish authorities. He was rewarded with 30 silver coins. They plotted to arrest Jesus by night, away from the crowds. Although the other disciples swore undying allegiance, Jesus warned that they too would abandon him. His prophecy was sadly fulfilled.

After their meal, they sang a hymn and walked to a garden called Gethsemane on the Mount of Olives. Jesus knew what was coming. He prayed with deep emotion, asking that he might be spared the dreadful suffering which the next few hours would bring. But his prayer ended with these famous words, '... *yet not my will, but yours be done*' (Luke 22:42). Shortly after this, Jesus was arrested and interrogated through the night by hastily convened Jewish and Roman courts.

Rabble-rousers stirred up the people. No longer did the crowds cry 'Hosanna!' and 'Welcome!' Now they shouted 'Crucify!' Pontius Pilate, the Roman Procurator of Judaea (AD 26–36) wanted to release Jesus but gave way to the popular outcry. To distance himself from this decision he washed his hands in public (Matthew 27:24).

Jesus was stripped. Nails were driven through his hands and feet. The cross was raised, and he was left hanging between two criminals. Soldiers gambled for his single worldly possession: a seamless robe. Later, his side was pierced with a spear to ensure that he was dead. As he was dying, Jesus uttered seven sentences which are recorded in the four Gospels. Among these is his astonishing prayer: '*Father, forgive them, for they know not what they are doing.*'

A startling contrast

Blandina was a Christian who had the misfortune to live in Lyons in Gaul (modern France) in AD 77. The authorities wished to stamp out the Church. The job was straightforward: they had to persuade the Christians to disown their God and swear by the pagan gods.

Eusebius, an early historian (c. 260–c. 340), recorded these events. Blandina, he reported, wore out her tormentors with her endurance. So they put her back in prison. Later, they brought her into the arena, together with a 15-year-old boy called Ponticus. After he had been killed, they put Blandina in a net and presented her to a bull. 'And so', wrote Eusebius, 'she travelled herself along the same path of conflicts as they (her fellow martyrs) did, and hastened to them rejoicing and exulting in her departure.'

The peace and serenity, and the sense of the presence of God displayed by Blandina, is characteristic of the Christian martyrs since the time of Stephen. *It is in sharp contrast to the death of Jesus himself.*

In the Passion Narratives in the Gospels (e.g. Mark 14:32–15:47):

* We find a *lack* of serenity: 'He began to be deeply distressed and troubled.'
* We find a *lack* of peace: 'My soul is overwhelmed with sorrow.'
* We find a desire for escape: 'Abba, Father, everything is possible for you, take this cup from me.'
* We even find a sense of abandonment by God, as Jesus quotes the opening line of Psalm 22: 'My God, my God, why have you forsaken me?'

Jesus was no less courageous than the martyrs who followed him. He could have escaped to safe obscurity. Instead, he pressed on to Jerusalem, to his fatal confrontation with the authorities. But the striking contrast remains. *For those who died for Jesus Christ – a constant sense of the presence of God. For Jesus as he died – a sense of abandonment by God and of utter loneliness.* The martyrs faced death willingly; Jesus shrank from it.

Add to this the fact that those who followed Jesus to martyrdom drew their inspiration from his death, and we have a remarkable puzzle. It is a puzzle to which the New Testament gives a solution. The answer given there is that, for Jesus, there was an *extra factor*. The martyrs suffered physically; Jesus suffered *physically and spiritually*, as he experienced separation from God the Father for the first time in his life.

The martyrs bore *pain* for him; he bore *sin* for them: not only their own sin but the sin of the whole world. And it is sin which separates from God – hence the cry of abandonment from the cross. All this was summed up by John the Baptist when he referred to Jesus as 'the Lamb of God, who takes away the sin of the world' (John 1:29).

Light from a dark place

The death of Jesus Christ takes us to the heart of the Christian understanding of salvation. It is, according to St Paul, of 'first importance' (1 Corinthians 15:3). John Polkinghorne, former Professor of Mathematical Physics at Cambridge University, sums it up:

> *In that lonely figure in the dark, in the spent force of a deserted man dying on a cross, they see not the ultimate triumph of evil or futility but the only source of hope for mankind. 'God was in Christ reconciling the world to himself' (2 Corinthians 5:19) ... The crucifixion was not something which got out of hand, a tragic mistake which marred an otherwise wonderful life. On the contrary, it was the inevitable fulfilment of the life, purposed by God.*

> (*The Way the World Is*, SPCK)

Why was it necessary for Jesus to die to gain our salvation? This is a deep mystery. Indeed, St Paul admits that the notion of a man dying on a cross to save the world, appears very foolish (1 Corinthians 1:18–25). It cannot be fully understood; it can only be proclaimed – and believed or denied. But this mystery sheds light upon, and brings meaning to, countless lives.

The cross reveals the demands of Christian discipleship

We all have to choose between two ways of being crazy; the foolishness of the gospel and the nonsense of the values of this world.

(Jean Vanier)

'Follow me', said Jesus. Then he took the road to crucifixion. As baptism indicates, following Christ always involves a sort of death. It means trying to hold Christian standards in a world which often rejects those standards. It means following Jesus in a world which is often indifferent towards him. Jesus summed up like this: 'If any want to become my followers, let them deny themselves and take up their cross and follow me' (Mark 8:34).

Paradoxically, Jesus insists that the cross is also about *life*. He goes on to say, 'For those who want to save their life will lose it, and those who lose their life for my sake, and for the sake of the gospel, will save it.'

George McLeod founded the modern Iona Community in Scotland. His words remind us that the crucifixion of Jesus is not just a terrible but fascinating incident in history, nor a puzzle in theology, nor simply an object for adoration and art. It is a constant challenge to all who seek to follow the crucified Christ:

> *I simply argue that the cross be raised again at the centre of the marketplace as well as on the steeple of the church. I am recovering the claim that Jesus was not crucified in a cathedral between two candles, but on a cross between two thieves; on the town garbage heap; at a crossroads so cosmopolitan that they had to write his title in Hebrew and Latin and in Greek ... at the kind of place where cynics talk smut, and thieves curse, and soldiers gamble. Because this is where he died. And this is what he died about. And that is where churchmen ought to be and what churchmen should be about.*

Rather than using his power to dominate, Jesus chose to submit himself to human wickedness. So the power of God is seen in symbols of weakness: a borrowed manger for his birth and a wooden cross at his death. Here is power kept in check; power handed over; power utterly controlled by love.

> *Jews demand miraculous signs and Greeks look for wisdom,*
> *but we preach Christ crucified: a stumbling-block to Jews and*
> *foolishness to Gentiles ... For the foolishness of God is wiser*
> *than man's wisdom, and the weakness of God is stronger than*
> *man's strength.*

> (1 Corinthians 1:22–25)

The apostle Paul wrote those words after his conversion to Jesus Christ. As Saul, he had persecuted the Church of Christ. In those days he *knew* that the Christians were wrong, because he knew the Hebrew Scriptures. Deuteronomy 21:22–23 is clear: 'anyone who is hung upon a tree is under God's curse'. Jesus had been crucified – hung upon a tree – therefore he was accursed. So he could not be the Messiah, as his followers claimed. This was the logic which had motivated Saul's persecution of the church.

Now renamed Paul, the apostle came to see that the cross was indeed the place of a curse. But the curse which Jesus bore was *ours*, not his. For he took upon himself the curse of human sin. So, with immense daring, Paul could write: 'Christ delivered us from the curse of the law, having become a curse for us' (Galatians 3:13).

So it was that Paul discovered and described the power of the cross in this vivid, perhaps shocking, way. Throughout the next 20 centuries, countless individuals would come to find its power by one route or another. This is captured by the historian G Kitson Clark, who ends his book *The Kingdom of Free Men* (Cambridge University Press) with these moving words:

> *So we have reached the end of our journey, and we have*
> *arrived at no pleasant place. It is in fact a place of public*
> *execution. Yet all human roads lead here in the end. This is*
> *the capital of the kingdom of free men and there, ruling*
> *from the gallows, is the King.*

3

risen Lord

Two profound questions are centre stage as we consider 'the human condition':

Is death the end of us? Do we simply bumble around on this planet only to disappear into Empty Nothingness when we die?

Are we on our own as we make our way through life? Or are we accompanied by a living Presence who guides, prompts, encourages and challenges us?

Christians believe that the joyful answers to these key questions are found in the resurrection of Jesus Christ. The source of our optimism and hope is captured in the jubilant liturgical affirmation which rings out around the globe on Easter Sunday:

Alleluia! Christ is risen.
He is risen indeed. Alleluia!

The great poet John Donne (Dean of St Paul's Cathedral 1621–31) caught this in his sonnet:

Death be not proud, though some have called thee
Mighty and dreadful, for, thou art not so …
One short sleep past, we wake eternally,
And death shall be no more. Death, thou shalt die.

The Acts of the Apostles describes a visit made by the apostle Paul to Athens. As he spoke, some local philosophers asked, 'What is this babbler trying to say?' They were told that he seemed to be speaking about foreign gods, 'because Paul was preaching the good news about Jesus and the resurrection' (Acts 17:18). As they half-listened, Paul's hearers thought that he was talking about two deities (*Jesus* and *Anastasis* – the Greek word for resurrection), because they heard these two words so frequently linked together.

This stress on Jesus and his resurrection is found throughout the New Testament. The 21 Letters were written in the conviction that Jesus is alive. The Acts of the Apostles contains sermons which declare that God raised Jesus from the dead. The Gospels end, not with the death and burial of Jesus, but with accounts of the way in which he appeared to his disciples.

We will consider just one of these stories: the appearance of Jesus to Mary Magdalene. St John tells us (John 20:1) that Mary went to the garden tomb very early on the first day of the week, only to find the stone removed from the entrance. She alerted two disciples, Peter and John, who inspected the empty tomb and then returned home.

Mary remained and encountered an angel and a man. Thinking that the man was the gardener, Mary asked if he had moved the body. But according to the fourth Gospel, Mary was not talking to a gardener – she was talking to a carpenter. It was Jesus himself, risen from the dead. Jesus addressed Mary by name and she recognized him. He instructed her to tell his followers ('my brothers') about their meeting. Mary went to the disciples with her exciting news: 'I have seen the Lord.'

This story focuses on two important features which occur frequently in the Gospels:
  * the tomb was empty
  * the risen Lord appeared to one (usually more than one) of his followers.

The centrality of the resurrection

The resurrection of Jesus Christ is not just one aspect of Christianity. We cannot remove a portion of the Christian jigsaw labelled 'resurrection' and leave anything which is recognizable as Christian faith. Subtract the resurrection and you destroy the entire picture. Indeed, without the resurrection of Jesus from the dead, it is unlikely that we would have a trace of his teaching, or anything else in the New Testament.

In the early Church there was no preaching about Jesus except as risen Lord. Nor could there be. For without the Apostles' conviction that they had seen Jesus alive again after his crucifixion, there would have been no preaching at all. There would have been deep mourning for a lost friend and great admiration for a dead hero. No doubt his profound teaching would have been remembered and cherished by his small, loyal circle of followers. But when they died, he would have been forgotten. Significantly, the early Christian preachers were less concerned to expound his teaching than to declare his death and resurrection.

The assertion that a man who was dead and buried has been raised up from the grave is breathtaking: those who make such a claim must give their reasons. In this chapter, some important facts will be set out and their possible implications discussed. Readers may consider the evidence to be strong or weak. Certainly it is not overwhelming. There will always be some who will assert that something as extraordinary as resurrection simply could not have happened, however strong the evidence might appear to be.

The Gospel accounts of the post-resurrection appearances of Jesus are striking in this regard. They provide readers with space in which to doubt, to question and to explore. For they freely admit that the disciples themselves found the whole thing very difficult to accept. St Matthew tells us that at the end of the 40 days during which Jesus appeared, 'some doubted' (Matthew 28:17). St Luke tells us that even with the risen Lord present, the disciples 'disbelieved for joy' (Luke 24:41). It was simply too good to be true!

The burning conviction which runs throughout the New Testament did not come easily.

In any case, evidence can take us only so far. We may sympathize with 'doubting Thomas' who reserved his judgement until he received convincing proof. But when he received the evidence which he requested, he did not simply say, 'So it is true.' Rather, he acknowledged the risen Christ as 'My Lord and my God!' (John 20:28). For Thomas, fact and evidence were followed by faith and commitment. With this in mind, we turn to some significant facts which cry out for adequate explanation.

Fact 1: No one produced the body

The Church began, not primarily by the spreading of ideas, but by the proclamation of a *fact*. Something has *happened*, said the apostles: God has raised Jesus from the dead. Those who wanted to discredit the apostles – and the Jewish leaders wanted to do that very much indeed – had only to produce one piece of evidence. *All they had to do was produce the body of Jesus. If they had done so, we would never have heard of him or his followers. There would be no New Testament and no Church.*

It is very significant that they did not do this. If the authorities had taken the body, or discovered it still in the tomb – because the disciples had lied, or gone to the wrong grave – they would have produced the corpse. This would have silenced all talk of resurrection. Instead, the authorities imprisoned, threatened, and beat the disciples. And they circulated the report that the disciples had stolen the body. It is clear that the Jewish and Roman leaders had no idea what had happened to Jesus. Yet the stubborn fact remains: his body had gone.

Fact 2: The movement almost died

The Christian faith shares some common features with other great world religions. In particular, it looks back to a charismatic founder whose teaching is central for all his followers. In this it is like Buddhism, which traces back to Gautama the Buddha; and Islam, which owes so much to the energy, vision and inspiration of

Muhammad, the Prophet of Allah. But when all the similarities have been noted, the *differences* between Jesus and other great religious leaders are startling and puzzling. Three in particular are relevant to this chapter:

1 Jesus died very young:
  - Gautama the Buddha died *c.* 483 BC, aged 80;
  - Muhammad died in AD 632, aged 62;
  - Jesus died *c.* AD 33, while only in his 30s.
2 Jesus spent no more than three years in the public eye.
3 When Jesus died, the movement which he founded was in rapid decline.

Movements do grow and develop after the founder's death; we have ample evidence of this. It happens when the founder leaves a growing movement. And it happens when the founder's followers are in a buoyant frame of mind, because everything depends on their 'get-up-and-go'. When Jesus died, these two factors were conspicuously absent. His followers were dwindling in number; those who remained were dispirited and afraid.

Yet somehow this demoralized group experienced a remarkable turn-around. Within a few weeks they were full of creative energy. They launched the biggest movement the world has ever seen, and one of the eventual fruits of this remarkable turn-around was the New Testament. *In other words, it was the resurrection of Jesus which gave the teaching of Jesus to the world.*

No resurrection; no record of his teaching.

Jesus' disciples gave two reasons for their own remarkable transformation, and these reasons have been celebrated ever since, in two great Christian festivals.

Easter The first disciples claimed that God had raised Jesus from the dead. Because this happened on a Sunday, they transferred their 'special' day from the traditional Jewish Sabbath (the last day of the week) to the first day. This change is in itself a remarkable fact, requiring adequate explanation. For Christians, every Sunday is a 'mini-Easter'.

Pentecost (sometimes called Whitsun) The first disciples claimed that God had given them the gift of his Holy Spirit.

They affirmed that it was God's Spirit within them who gave them boldness, joy and insight.

Fact 3: The disciples suffered for their preaching

'Then all the disciples deserted him and fled.' In this short sentence, Matthew describes the behaviour of the disciples of Jesus following his arrest. He goes on to tell of the way in which Peter, for all his earlier boasting, denied all knowledge of Jesus. In the circumstances, such behaviour was completely understandable. However, a few weeks later those men were out in the streets, preaching that God had raised Jesus from the dead. These were the same men who had deserted him. They were the same men who had been shattered by his crucifixion. But as the Acts of the Apostles makes very clear, they were very different same men!

In place of bitter disappointment there was joyful confidence; in place of fear there was boldness. Instead of thinking gloomily that their leader was dead, they proclaimed that he had conquered death. In other words, they were transformed. The question is: what transformed them? They claimed that it was their experience of the risen Lord.

An invention?

This possibility is undermined by one significant fact: history and human psychology teach us that people will suffer for deeply held convictions. However, nobody is prepared to suffer for an invention. We tell lies to get *out* of trouble, not to get *into* it. The whip and the sword soon uncover fraud. Besides, liars do not usually write high-calibre moral literature like the New Testament.

Did Jesus really die?

The willing suffering of the disciples also rules out the 'swoon' theory. On this view, Jesus did not die on the cross. Despite terrible wounds, he recovered in the tomb and escaped. The disciples nursed him back to health, or tried to and failed.

This theory bristles with problems. Roman soldiers knew when a man was dead; and there was a guard on the tomb. But if we allow that somehow the disciples overcame these problems, the events which follow simply do not fit. Jesus would have cheated death; he would not have *conquered* it. No doubt the disciples would have been delighted, but they would have kept the whole thing very quiet. *Publicity and preaching would have been fatal*, for these would have resulted in a search. The authorities would not have made a second mistake.

Besides, to preach that God had raised Jesus from the dead – which is exactly what they *did* preach – would have been a lie. We are back where we started. The lash, the dungeon and the sword would soon have loosened their tongues. People will suffer and die for their *convictions*, but not for their inventions.

Fact 4: Eyewitnesses were available

In his first letter to the Corinthians, Paul lists various eyewitnesses – people who had seen the risen Lord, who were still alive when he wrote and who could be questioned. This list includes a crowd of 'more than 500'. Free invention for purposes of propaganda could have been checked and contradicted.

Fact 5: Jesus is called Lord

The early disciples were Jews – devout monotheists who frequently recited the *Shema*: 'The Lord our God, the Lord is one' (Deuteronomy 6:4). Then they met Jesus or heard about him in sermons and conversations.

At no point did they abandon their belief in One God. It would have been unthinkable for them to become 'bi-theists' (believers in two gods). Yet their concept of God was greatly enlarged as a result of their contact with Jesus. So, while continuing to assert that God is One, they began to speak of God the Father and God the Son. Indeed, shortly after his death they had firmly placed Jesus, the man from Nazareth, on the *Godward* side of that line which divides humanity from divinity. They did not doubt that he was truly human, but they offered him their worship.

How can this amazing shift in attitude be explained? How can we account for the fact that those Jewish men and women (some of whom knew Jesus personally, and all of whom knew that he was a man who sweated and wept) addressed him as *Lord*?

Jewish men and women would have been incapable of *deciding* to use the word 'Lord' in that way. Their entire upbringing was against it, because it carried a huge risk of being blasphemous. No, it was forced upon them – partly by the teaching of Jesus but mainly by their conviction that God had raised Jesus from the dead. They quickly came to realize that if Jesus was Lord over death, he was quite simply ... 'LORD'.

Fact 6: Significant witnesses endorse it

In a court of law, expert and surprising witnesses are sometimes called: those with special expertise in the subject under consideration, or people whose background and insights might lead the jury to expect them to come down on the opposite side. One such witness is the mathematical physicist Professor John Polkinghorne. As a physicist he might be expected to disbelieve in such an extraordinary miracle as resurrection, which appears to contravene the laws of nature. In fact he understands this in terms of 'regime change' – a scientific concept which he applies to the resurrection of Jesus (fuller details are on the CD *Science and Christian Faith* www.yorkcourses.co.uk). Other surprising and significant witnesses in this investigation are *Jewish* scholars with no Christian axe to grind.

Implications

Christians believe that the resurrection of Jesus from the dead has enormous implications. At least two are clear, and extremely practical.

Death is dead

Our mortality exercises a profound influence upon us – producing a range of responses from fear to curiosity. Most reflective people occasionally feel the need to consider the fact that they will die, and the related need to attempt to make sense of life in the light of this inevitable but awesome fact.

The words of Jesus, as recorded in the fourth Gospel, are breathtaking in their sweep:

> *I am the resurrection and the life. He who believes in me will live, even though he dies; and whoever lives and believes in me will never die. Do you believe this?*
>
> (John 11:25, 26)

Here is the highest arrogance and folly, or the most profound wisdom. Which of these alternatives is true, depends upon the truth or otherwise of the resurrection of Jesus himself.

Jesus is alive

Countless believers from all cultures and personality types testify to a sense of being 'accompanied' through life by a 'presence' which, though unseen, is very real. This presence, they affirm, is a Person – the risen Christ. They claim that he challenges, guides, encourages, inspires and renews them. Their experience is captured by the great (and controversial) Albert Schweitzer (1875–1965), a radical theologian and brilliant musicologist. He abandoned his outstanding academic career to train as a doctor, in order to go to West Africa as a missionary. Albert Schweitzer wrote:

> *He comes to us as one unknown, without a name, as of old by the lakeside. He came to those men who knew Him not. He speaks to us the same word: 'Follow thou me!' and sets us to the tasks which He has to fulfil for our time. He commands. And to those who obey Him, whether they be wise or simple, He will reveal himself in the toils, the conflicts, the suffering which they shall pass through in His fellowship, and, as an ineffable mystery, they shall learn in their own experience Who He is.*
>
> (*The Quest of the Historical Jesus*, SCM Press)

4

the Bible

The broadcaster and novelist, Melvyn Bragg wrote these remarkable words: '*probably the most influential book that's ever been in the history of language – English or any other*'.

Was he writing about Shakespeare? Or a work of scientific brilliance, perhaps? He was in fact referring to William Tyndale's translation of the Bible into English.

The Bible continues to speak to millions in the modern world. It deals with the 'constants' in human life – with anguish and joy, with personal relationships, with our need to make sense of life. These timeless writings tell us about men and women who worked, worried, loved, laughed, fought, forgave, suffered, grew old and died. They are about people like us.

These ancient Scriptures consider the great and abiding issues of life and death, sensitively and profoundly.

Martin Niemöller was a Christian Pastor imprisoned under the Nazis. For his opposition to Hitler he suffered solitary confinement and spent four years in Dachau concentration camp. Afterwards, he reflected on the importance of the Bible to him during those long years:

The Word of God was simply everything to me – comfort and strength, guidance and hope, master of my days and companion of my nights, the bread which kept me from starvation, and the water of life which refreshed my soul.

Brian Redhead was a popular British broadcaster. To prepare for a BBC series entitled *The Good Book* he read the Bible from cover to cover and commented:

It's really a journey through life. It makes sense of the universe we find ourselves in. The story line is tremendous. It just is the greatest document of the lot, and once you've read it, your life is never the same.

'Whoever made this book made me; it knows all that is in my heart.' (a Chinese reader of the Bible)

'The Bible is the cradle in which Christ is laid.' (Martin Luther)

'For Christians, the Bible centres on Christ – the New Testament being explicitly about him, the Old foretelling him.' (Professor Ninian Smart)

One Bible, two Testaments

The Christian Bible is divided into two unequal parts. The New Testament (or Covenant) contains 27 'books'; the Old Testament contains 39 books and is far longer. It is highly significant that on accepting Jesus as the great new act of God, the early Christians did not feel that the Hebrew Scriptures were redundant. They had been *fulfilled*, not replaced.

The Old Testament contains a rich variety of styles: story, history, law, poetry, lament, reflection ... The New Testament writers frequently drew from these older writings, especially the prophets and the psalms. Among Old Testament passages which are especially loved by Christian believers are Psalm 23 and Isaiah 53. The first Christians viewed the latter as a highly significant passage, pointing to – even describing in detail – the crucifixion of Jesus (Acts 8:26–35).

The Old Testament prophets spoke about a *New Covenant* yet to come (Jeremiah 31:31). At the Last Supper which Jesus ate with his disciples, he made it clear that this New Covenant was about to be sealed in the terrible events to follow. Thus, for Christians, the two sections are held together: the Old pointing forward to the New; the New fulfilling the Old. It is also true that the New Testament marks a radical new beginning. There is *contrast* as well as *continuity*. Christians believe that the centre and fulcrum of it all is Jesus Christ – the light and hope of the world.

Remembering and recording

Jesus of Nazareth and his first disciples (all Jews) were conscious of standing in a long and noble tradition. It was a tradition in which the Scriptures had a central place. In his Gospel Luke tells us that Jesus went into the synagogue in his home town of Nazareth, where the people had gathered for worship on the Sabbath. He took a scroll of Hebrew Scripture and read from the prophet Isaiah:

> **The Spirit of the Lord is upon me, because he has anointed me to preach good news to the poor. He has sent me to proclaim freedom for the prisoners and recovery of sight for the blind, to release the oppressed, to proclaim the year of the Lord's favour.**
>
> (Luke 4:18, 19)

Jesus returned the scroll to the official and declared: '*Today has this prophecy been fulfilled in your hearing.*'

Jesus constantly drew on the Hebrew Scriptures, bringing out deeper meanings, making new connections and – astonishing to his hearers – claiming to be the One to whom the Hebrew prophets pointed. This notion of Jesus fulfilling the rich promises and prophecies scattered throughout the Old Testament, became a key theme for the writers of the New Testament.

Scrolls represented weeks of careful work by authors or scribes. The development of the *codex* (a book with a spine) by the fourth century AD would bring a minor revolution, but scrolls carried the first written accounts of the good news about Jesus Christ.

Many scrolls were communal property which were read out to the assembled company. In addition, unrecorded stories were passed on by word of mouth. This is how the stories about Jesus, and accounts of his teaching, circulated in the days of his ministry and in the months and years following his death. Teaching, preaching, storytelling; hearing, remembering, repeating: these were crucial elements in the spread of the message of Jesus and his early followers. The oral and the written accounts intermingled at an early stage.

Which languages?

Eventually the first disciples grew old, or their lives were in danger from persecution. The need for a written record of the actions and teaching of Jesus became urgent. In a remarkably short time, the four Gospels which stand at the beginning of the New Testament came into being – written in Greek.

Jesus and his first disciples were almost certainly tri-lingual. They spoke Aramaic and a few Aramaic words are scattered throughout the New Testament. They understood Hebrew, the language of their own Jewish Scriptures. But to communicate widely they also needed Greek, the language spoken and written throughout the Roman Empire. This is the language of the New Testament.

Why these books?

The first few Christian centuries gave rise to a considerable volume of literature. So two questions arise: why and how did these particular 27 books come to comprise the New Testament?

In the early Church, the term 'Scripture' originally referred to writings from the Old Testament. But the second letter of Peter refers to Paul's letters as Scripture and very soon Christian writers, such as Justin Martyr (c. 100–165), were referring to 'the New Testament'. For some time there was debate about whether certain books should be included (for example, hesitations were expressed about Hebrews, 2 Peter and Jude). In the Armenian Church, the inclusion of Revelation was resisted until the twelfth century.

Some other early writings, such as the *Didache* and the *First Letter of Clement*, were serious contenders for inclusion. There was also some disagreement about the *order* of the books. The four Gospels and Paul's letters were accepted as authoritative by the end of the second century. In AD 367, Bishop Athanasius wrote a letter in which he listed the 27 books of the New Testament as being canonical, i.e. official Scripture.

Reliable manuscripts?

Existing ancient documents have survived a hazardous journey down the centuries. They were written and copied by hand (a slow and laborious process) and were liable to damage or destruction by fire, water, rough usage or simple neglect. So it comes as no surprise to learn that the world's museums and libraries contain only:

* eight ancient copies of *Thucydides' History*
* ten ancient copies of *Caesar's Gallic War*
* two ancient copies of the *Histories of Tacitus*.

By ancient copies we mean that there is a gap of about 1300, 900 and 700 years respectively, between the originals of these famous historical documents and the copies which have survived. In contrast, hundreds of ancient copies of the Gospels can be found in the world's museums and libraries. So it is evident that there is a rich harvest of ancient biblical texts for scholars to work with.

The wealth of manuscripts, and above all the narrow interval of time between the writing and the earliest extant copies, make it by far the best-attested text of any ancient writing in the world.

(John Robinson)

The New Testament manuscripts in our possession are much closer in time to the original writings, more numerous and in closer agreement with each other than any other ancient book.

(Professor Hans Küng)

In the end, of course, we weigh all the available evidence and decide to trust the records — or not, as the case may be. Professor David Ford puts the Christian position with great clarity:

The Gospels are testimony. Because we cannot re-run historical events, you either have to trust or not trust some of the people who were there. It is important that we as Christians are part of a community that did decide early on to trust certain testimonies. That does not rule them out from cross-examination. But we can be absolutely confident that in terms of the testimony of Jesus, there is no disproof of the main thrust of that testimony.

Hundreds of early copies of parts of the New Testament are available to scholars. Two complete copies of the New Testament are dated around AD 350 — less than 300 years after the original. One is in the Vatican Library; the other in the British Museum. The latter was bought from the Soviet Government on Christmas Day 1933 for £100,000. The earliest undisputed find, a fragment from St John's Gospel, is dated around AD 130 and is held in the John Rylands Library in Manchester.

The Dead Sea Scrolls

From time to time an archaeological find, or a new theory, makes headlines because it gives rise to sensational claims which appear to disprove established ideas. One famous example is the Dead Sea Scrolls. These scrolls were from the library of a Jewish community based at Qumran on the north-western shore of the Dead Sea, between 150 BC and AD 68. Their discovery in 1947 was described by Professor W F Albright as 'the greatest manuscript discovery of modern times'.

Wild claims were made for the Scrolls. In particular, a few writers suggested that there were strong similarities between Jesus and the original leader (*The Teacher of Righteousness*) of the community which wrote and preserved the scrolls. It was argued that Christianity had its roots in the teaching of this Jewish sect, which flourished before Jesus was born. A group of scholars working on the Scrolls denied this. They issued a statement asserting that: '*Nothing that appears in the scrolls hitherto discovered throws any doubts on the originality of Christianity.*' There is a marked contrast between:

* the Community at Qumran (where the scrolls were found) and the early Christians
* the Teacher of Righteousness and Jesus.

This contrast was later confirmed by two Jewish scholars: Geza Vermes and Yigael Yadin. The position is summed up by the British archaeologist, Professor Alan Millard: '*The differences between the Teacher of Righteousness and Jesus are huge.*'

This does not detach Jesus from his culture. There *are* similarities between Jesus and other Jewish teachers of his day. As we have seen, Jesus was unique in approach and stature but he did not set out to be 'original'. He gladly accepted many of the rich traditions of his nation and was aware of standing within the flow of its history.

Pursuing links between Jesus and the Teacher of Righteousness may have ended in a cul-de-sac, but the Dead Sea Scrolls do have some bearing upon the Bible: both Old and New Testaments.

The Scrolls increase our confidence in the text of the Old Testament. At least part of every Old Testament book (except Esther) has been found in the Scrolls. They are about 1,000 years older than any other text of the Hebrew Scriptures so far discovered.

Careful comparison shows just how successful Jewish scribes were, over the centuries, in their desire to pass on faithful and accurate copies of the Scriptures. Magnus Magnusson rightly spoke of 'the essential integrity of the scribal tradition'.

The Scrolls illuminate the world of the New Testament, for they were written between 150 BC and AD 68. Before the Scrolls were discovered, some scholars believed that John's Gospel was a free composition, written in the second century under Greek influence. If so, it had no strong roots in history. But when we put the Dead Sea Scrolls alongside the fourth Gospel, we see how very Jewish St John's work is. Contrasts like 'light and dark' and 'life and death', which abound in John's Gospel, were thought to be Greek in origin. The Dead Sea Scrolls show that these contrasts are at home in first-century Jewish thought. So the fourth Gospel fits well into the Jewish background which it describes; it has a secure basis in the history of that period.

In 2007 Professor Michael Jursa of the British Museum deciphered an ancient cuneiform inscription on a clay tablet dating from 595 BC, confirming a payment by Nabu-sharrussu-ukin, 'chief eunuch' at the court of King Nebuchadnezzar. He commented, 'A throwaway detail in the Old Testament turns out to be accurate and true. I think that means that the whole of the narrative [of the prophet Jeremiah] takes on a new kind of power.'

Translations

An estimated 6,900 languages and major dialects are spoken around the world. But many of these are spoken by minority groups who are often competent in at least one other mainstream language. At the beginning of 2008, the number of languages with a translation of some or all of the Bible reached 2,426. In 2006 the complete Bible was available in 429 languages and the New Testament had been translated into a further 1,144. This means that at least part of the Bible is available to the vast majority of nations, tribes and clans.

The first book to be printed using moveable type was the *Gutenberg Bible* in 1456. This was the Old Latin version by Jerome (342–420) called the *Vulgate*. The world's presses continue to print hundreds of thousands of copies of the Bible, which remains the world's best-seller (even though copies are often given away free of charge). English translations abound; among the most famous are:

* *Tyndale's Translation*, which was based on Hebrew and Greek manuscripts. It is incomplete, because William Tyndale was executed in 1536 before he finished his great work. It formed the basis for the Authorized Version. Tyndale's work is 'probably the most influential book that's ever been in the history of language – English or any other' (Melvyn Bragg).

* The *Geneva Bible*, which was dedicated to Queen Elizabeth I who came to the throne in 1558. This Bible introduced the verse numbers that are now in universal use. Before this, only chapter divisions had been available.

* The *Authorized Version* (or King James Version) of 1611, which established itself as *the* English edition for 300 years. It is still in use but many regular Bible readers use modern editions. These are easier to understand and based on more numerous and accurate sources.

Moving stories are told of churches where Bibles are scarce. The Scriptures are treasured, memorized, copied and circulated with great care and love. By their commitment these believers declare with the Psalmist that:

The ordinances of the Lord are sure
and altogether righteous.
They are more precious than gold,
than much pure gold.

(Psalm 19:9, 10)

Euangelio (that we cal gospel) is a greke worde, and signyfyth good, mery, glad and joyfull tydings, that maketh a mannes hert glad, and maketh hym syngge, daunce and leepe for joye.

William Tyndale, Bible translator

5

Christian experience of God

When I look back at those days, I have no doubt that Providence guided us, not only across those snowfields, but across the storm-white sea that separated Elephant Island from our landing-place on South Georgia. I know that during that long and racking march of thirty-six hours over the unnamed mountains and glaciers of South Georgia, it seemed to me often that we were four, not three. I said nothing to my companions on the point, but afterwards Worsley said to me, 'Boss, I had a curious feeling on the march that there was another person with us.'

Ernest Shackleton in *South* (1919)

Research into religious experience was pioneered by the zoologist, Sir Alister Hardy. It has revealed that spiritual experiences are much more common than is often supposed. Best known are so-called 'near death experiences', but there are many others, as the above quotation from the Antarctic explorer illustrates. In this chapter we shall consider the transforming nature of such experiences.

Starting with the Bible

The Bible is full of people who claim to have had an experience of God.

Somewhat similar experiences have been recorded throughout Christian history. Some have become famous; others are known to only a few. In this chapter we shall consider a tiny sample, to illustrate the breadth of the Christian experience of God.

Conversion

The human heart is heavy and hardened. God must give a man a new heart. Conversion is first of all a work of the grace of God who makes our hearts turn to him ... God gives us the strength to begin anew.

(Catechism of the Catholic Church)

Malcolm Worsley was a thief. On the day of yet another release from prison, a prison officer remarked, 'You'll be back, Worsley.' That officer was right; Malcolm did return, but as a member of staff! For in prison, Malcolm had been converted to Christ. He trained to be a probation officer, and worked with people who are dependent on drugs. In July 1996, Malcolm was ordained as a minister in the Church of England.

Metropolitan **Anthony Bloom** was different from Malcolm Worsley in almost every way: education, personality, upbringing and culture. In turn he became a surgeon, a member of the resistance movement in the Second World War and leader of the Russian Orthodox Church in Britain. He too had a remarkable experience which gave shape and direction to his future life.

As a teenager he wanted to prove to himself that Christianity was untrue, so he read St Mark's Gospel. (He chose St Mark because it is the shortest, and he didn't want to waste time on the exercise!) He wrote:

Before I reached the third chapter, I suddenly became aware that on the other side of my desk there was a presence. And the certainty was so strong that it was Christ standing

there that it has never left me. This was the real turning point.
Because Christ was alive and I had been in his presence
I could say with certainty that what the Gospel said about
the crucifixion of the prophet of Galilee was true, and the
centurion was right when he said, 'truly he is the Son of God'.

(*School for Prayer*, DLT)

There are two further points to note about conversion. First, the phrase 'conversion of life'. Many writers on spirituality insist that conversion is a process. *Every day* we need to do battle with temptation and turn to Christ. Second, Christian discipleship does not depend upon dramatic experiences. From the New Testament we learn that Timothy (a younger colleague of the apostle Paul) came to faith gradually through the influence of a Christian home (2 Timothy 1:5; 2 Timothy 3:15). Research suggests that a minority of Christians have a dramatic conversion experience. The way into faith is less important than the outcome. David L Edwards makes this point clearly and helpfully:

That is why everyone is challenged to respond to God through
Jesus Christ in a personal turning (which is what the word
'conversion' means). You have to meet Jesus yourself, and to
accept him as your friend and as your Lord ... In many Christian
lives, this turning or conversion reaches a climax which can
be dated. People can remember the exact time when they
accepted Jesus Christ as Lord and Liberator, often after
intense struggles to escape from the pressure of his love. But it
is not necessary to be able to date your conversion like that.

What is essential is that everyone should have his or her
personal reasons for being a Christian. You cannot inherit
Christian faith as you can inherit red hair or a peculiar nose.
You cannot copy Christian faith as you can copy hairstyle or
an accent. And you cannot get it completely out of books, as
you can get a knowledge of history.

Your faith, to be authentic, to guide your life, must be your
own. Your very own experience, whether it is dramatic or
quiet, long or short, must lead you to know Jesus Christ as
your personal liberator.

(*What Anglicans Believe*, Mowbray)

Guidance

Frances Young is a university professor and a mother. She teaches theology, and returns home to a severely disabled son. Frances is a radical, probing theologian, who knows that there are no knockdown arguments for the existence of God. Yet she speaks with deep conviction of her own faith, and about certain experiences which convince her of the reality of a personal God.

One day she was sitting in a chair when she had a 'loud thought'. It was as though a voice said to her, 'It doesn't make any difference to Me whether you believe in Me or not!' Later, when driving her car, she had another 'loud thought' telling her to be ordained. She cannot remember the journey itself ('I must have been on automatic pilot or something!') but she remembers the experience very clearly.

> *I had the whole of my life laid out in front of me; and all its peculiar twists and turns which hadn't seemed to make very much sense suddenly fell into a pattern, as though this was all leading up to that moment and that conclusion. It was quite dramatic in its way.*

Frances was ordained as a minister in the Methodist Church on 3 July 1984.

Alexander Solzhenitsyn, the Russian novelist, also believed that he received a commission from God for his life's work. As a young dissident he was imprisoned by the Soviet authorities. In his memoir *The Oak and the Calf* he described his despair at being told that, because of cancer, he had only three weeks to live. He had so much to tell the world and he feared that the Soviet authorities would discover and destroy his writings. Desperately he hid his work (in champagne bottles!). That was in 1953. In 1970 he won the Nobel Prize for literature. He commented:

> *With a hopelessly neglected and acutely malignant tumour, this was a divine miracle; I could see no other explanation. Since then all the life that had been given back to me has not been mine in the full sense: it is built around a purpose.*

Prayer, protection and reassurance

A remarkable example of God apparently answering prayer, has been recounted by the Russian poet **Irina Ratushinskaya**. Irina spent four years in Soviet prisons and labour camps for her literary and human rights activities, before being released in 1986. In a poem, Irina describes herself as 'a huddle by an icy wall'. This gives a sense of the biting cold, the inadequate clothing and the poor diet. But she testifies to two kinds of warmth which she sometimes experienced: the inner emotional warmth of joy and a physical warmth throughout her body, despite the freezing conditions. It is her conviction that these phenomena (experienced by other prisoners, too) were a direct answer to prayer, as this extract from one of her poems shows.

> *Believe me, it was often thus*
> *In solitary cells, on winter nights*
> *A sudden sense of joy and warmth*
> *And a resounding note of love.*
> *And then, unsleeping, I would know*
> *A huddle by an icy wall:*
> *Someone is thinking of me now,*
> *Petitioning the Lord for me.*

from: *Pencil Letter* (Hutchinson)

Gerald Priestland was a distinguished BBC Foreign Affairs correspondent. Following a breakdown, he underwent psychoanalysis and moved from atheism to belief in God. He became a Quaker. Gerald once said, 'I hope I believe. I know that I trust.' His faith, his doubts and his questions were essential tools for his next job as BBC Religious Affairs correspondent.

In 1991 Gerald suffered a stroke. In one of his last broadcasts, his voice marked by a slur resulting from the stroke, he spoke these moving words:

> *I have had the feeling of being crushed under a rock till I could*
> *see only one crack of light, and that was the love of God, the*
> *absolute certainty, when everything else had been taken from*
> *me, that God loved me.*

Mysticism

Can the above experiences properly be described as 'mystical'? Professor Owen Chadwick defines mysticism as 'an experience of direct communication with God. It is not, for example, reading about Jesus and saying that is what God must be like: but kneeling down to say a prayer and suddenly feeling God there, facing you or beside you or in you'. He goes on to say that while people often attempt to describe such experiences, they all acknowledge the inadequacy of words to capture them. Other writers point out that while such experiences can be accompanied by a sense of ecstasy, this is not always the case. It is clear, therefore, that most of the experiences described above could be called 'mystical' – although the people involved might not wish to use that term. Such phenomena have been experienced by Christians throughout the centuries and some have become famous.

Blaise Pascal (1623–62)

A mathematician and scientist of great stature, Pascal is as famous for his theological writing as for his scientific work. In particular, his *Pensées* (*Thoughts on Religion and Some Other Subjects*) are still read today. On a 'Night of Fire' he experienced the reality of 'the God of Isaac, of Abraham and Jacob' (as opposed to the 'First Cause' God of the philosophers). He describes this in a series of vivid words: '*Fire … Certainty … Peace … Joy, tears of joy.*' He wrote, '*the heart has its reasons, of which reason knows nothing*'.

Daily life

As already indicated, the experiences outlined above are not confined to a few 'super-saints'. Large numbers of Christians could describe dramatic, 'out of the blue' spiritual experiences which have made a tremendous difference to the quality and direction of their lives. Sometimes they are life-transforming; frequently they leave the person involved with a quiet certainty about the reality and love of God.

But many other believers, probably the majority, do not have experiences of this kind. As a result, some feel 'second-class' in comparison. This is sad, for it is possible to have a strong faith in God without experiencing anything 'dramatic'. For some, the main pointer to the reality of God is a quiet confidence that they are 'accompanied', 'helped' and 'directed' through life by an unseen Presence – and challenged too, to acts of love and service.

In a famous sentence, Jesus promised his disciples that '*where two or three come together in my name, I am there in the midst of them*' (Matthew 18:20). Millions of ordinary believers, who have never had a 'special' encounter with God, testify that these words of Jesus sum up their experience. They affirm that they meet for prayer, worship and fellowship, not to remember a dead hero, but to meet – and to be met by – a living Person. Their testimony is impressive.

The importance of such undramatic experiences of God was captured by Cardinal Basil Hume, Archbishop of Westminster from 1976 to 1999:

> *Holiness involves friendship with God. God's love for us and ours for him grows like any relationship with other people. There comes a moment, which we can never quite locate or catch, when an acquaintance becomes a friend. In a sense, the change from one to the other has been taking place over a period of time, but there comes a point when we know we can trust the other, exchange confidences, keep each other's secrets. We are friends. There has to be a moment like that in our relationship with God. He ceases to be just a Sunday acquaintance and becomes a weekday friend.*
>
> (*To Be a Pilgrim*, SPCK)

Discipleship

As we have seen, powerful life-changing experiences are described in the Bible. And words of emotion, such as *joy* and *fear*, are often found there too. In the light of Christian belief in the resurrection of Jesus and the activity of the Holy Spirit, it is not surprising that experiences of God (whether gentle or dramatic) continue to be widespread. But all Christians would agree that the quality of our discipleship matters more than any particular spiritual experience.

What really counts is the response of the individual believer. Such experiences are 'given' for practical purposes: to broaden our understanding, to deepen our faith, to enlarge our compassion and to secure our obedience.

C S Lewis became a leading Christian 'apologist' (defender of the faith), part of whose story was told in the film *Shadowlands*. He was Professor of Medieval Literature at Oxford, and he wrote a series of famous children's books set in Narnia, including *The Lion, the Witch and the Wardrobe*. He also wrote science fiction, as well as many books about Christianity. He was converted from atheism after a long period of intellectual wrestling.

C S Lewis wrote a great deal about Christian faith, religious experience and obedience. He believed that God is often most obvious to the emotions and senses at the *beginning* of our Christian pilgrimage, to help get us started on our journey of faith. He argued that Christians sometimes make greater progress during periods when they have no direct sense of the presence of God. Only then are they really living 'by faith, not by sight' (2 Corinthians 5:7) – learning to trust the promises of God in the Bible, 'not in the teeth of reason, but in the teeth of lust, and terror, and jealousy and boredom and indifference'.

For Lewis, the *truth* of Christianity is everything. We are called to follow Jesus Christ whether we experience his presence or not, because he is 'the Way, the Truth and the Life' (John 14:6). He summed up his position like this:

> 'Christianity is a statement which, if false, is of no importance, and if true, of infinite importance. The one thing it cannot be is moderately important.'

The Doctrine of the Trinity

*May the grace of the Lord Jesus Christ, and the love of God,
and the fellowship of the Holy Spirit be with you all.*

(2 Corinthians 13:14)

The Christian doctrine that there are 'three Persons in one God' developed over the first few Christian centuries and is found in the Creeds hammered out at Church Councils: Nicaea (325), Constantinople (381) and Chalcedon (451). But the building blocks are found in the New Testament and in the experience of the early disciples. As they reflected on the significance of Jesus they became aware that he was 'the man Christ Jesus' (1 Timothy 2:5) *and* 'My Lord and my God' (John 20:28). On the day of Pentecost they were filled with the Holy Spirit. They understood these experiences as actions or manifestations of the One True God – Creator and Redeemer of the World.

The doctrine of the Trinity is linked with the Christian view of *revelation*. God is too good and too great for us to comprehend. But in his mercy he has revealed himself to us – in creation and through Scripture (prophets, poets, law, history, story ...). Supremely he has revealed himself in his Son (Hebrews 1:2) and by his Spirit within us (Galatians 5:22). It would have been impossible for the Jewish disciples of Jesus – with their tenacious belief that 'the Lord is One' – to *invent* this idea of One God as Father, Son and Holy Spirit. They were *forced* to this belief through their experience of Jesus, and the events of Easter and the first Christian Pentecost. This understanding of God as 'Three in One' was not worked out by lonely academics in libraries, but by men and women making sense of their experience in active lives and dangerous times.

The Doctrine of the Trinity makes God accessible. He is not locked away from us in heaven. God has become one of us in Jesus; he continues to live within us, and among us, by his Spirit.

6

prayer, worship and sacraments

Through prayer, believers seek to bring the needs of our broken and divided world to God – not because God is unaware of these needs, but because God wants to involve us in the world as peacemakers and healers.

Prayer does not replace action. It is a spur to practical concern – Christian compassion – as illustrated in the chapter on Church and Society.

Worship and prayer go beyond petition (prayers of asking) to encompass praise and thanksgiving, rejoicing and lament, confession and meditation.

In the sacraments of Baptism and Holy Communion, Christian worship focuses on events in the life of Jesus. From these we draw strength and inspiration and find ourselves empowered for life and service.

Prayer is not a matter of persuading God to do things which he might not want to do. Rather, it is a matter of aligning ourselves with his purpose. Even when (as is often the case) his will in detail is far from clear, the desire of the praying person is to bring his or her will into conformity with God's will; to want *his* will to be done.

The Khouds of North India have a prayer which reads: '*Lord, we don't know what is good for us. You know what it is. For it we pray. Amen*'. It is a prayer of confidence in God, a prayer which rests in his perfect, loving will. But what if we fear that we do not really want God's will to be done in some particular situation? Writers on prayer tell us that our 'fear' shows that we know we ought to want it. So they encourage us with the thought that God, who knows our hearts, mercifully accepts our *wanting to want it* and gently leads us into a fuller desire for it.

Jesus Christ taught his followers to pray to the Father, '*May your will be done on earth as it is in heaven*' (Matthew 6:10). From this we understand that the very best that could happen 'on earth' at any time, is that God's will should be done. Furthermore, the Holy Spirit is always at work, guiding those who genuinely want the will of God to be done. The confidence that God is active in the world (and will one day make all things new, permeating every part of his new creation with his glory), spurs the believer on to pray and work to make this world a better and a fairer place. This is in anticipation of the future consummation of God's Kingdom. So prayer is best thought of as an active response to the will of the God of history.

Aspects of prayer

There are various kinds of prayer.

Adoration and praise

The wonder of God's being and character evokes adoration. He is beyond our understanding; but he has revealed himself, supremely in Jesus Christ. God is seen as the One before whom heart and mind must bow, because in him is all perfection and beauty. Prayer may be expressed in words; but sometimes it goes beyond words into an attitude of silent and wordless devotion.

Thanksgiving

This is closely related to adoration. We reflect on everything which enriches our lives, sometimes giving thanks to God for specific blessings. But it does not stop there, for the whole work of God, past and present, occasions, thanksgiving.

Confession

This begins with an awareness that nobody is without sin in God's sight. In addition to 'sinfulness' (a shared failure to love God wholeheartedly and our neighbour as ourselves), there are particular sins of thought, word and deed to be acknowledged and repented of, if God's forgiveness is to be received and a fresh start made. While it is undesirable to 'rummage' in our lives to try to uncover every fault (as if this could be done), confessing particular known sins is important and can be therapeutic. However, in the course of Christian worship (i.e. worship in a Christian congregation) the prayer of confession must necessarily be general in character. The brief and beautiful 'Jesus Prayer' from the Eastern Orthodox tradition is used by many Christians: 'Lord Jesus Christ, Son of God, have mercy on me, a sinner.'

Many people find it helpful to share with another human being, in strict confidence, those things which are burdening their conscience. Some Christian traditions (such as Roman Catholic and Orthodox) commend the practice of personal confession to God in the presence of a priest. Some believers find that they come to an assurance of divine forgiveness more readily when they hear a declaration of that forgiveness from an authorized representative of the Church.

Intercession

This looks out at the world. It is the prayer of concern for individual people, groups of people, causes and events. Just why God should wish to involve us in his purposes through prayer, is a mystery. But, encouraged by Jesus' example and teaching about prayer, Christian believers gladly accept it as a mystery of love – and as a great privilege.

Lamentation

The Psalms cover the full range of human emotions, from joy to despair. These poems include deep expressions of sorrow and

sharp questions to God about his apparent silence and inactivity
(e.g. Psalms 10 and 13). In this way we are encouraged to be totally
honest in prayer, telling God 'how it is for us'.

Extemporary prayer

Over the centuries, thousands of written prayers have been
composed for all the above modes of prayer. Some are very
beautiful; some very famous. But many Christians use *extemporary*
(or *extempore*) prayer – praying in their own words rather than
from a written text. In some traditions (such as Roman Catholic,
Orthodox, Anglican) written prayers are usually preferred in public
worship. In others (such as Baptist and Pentecostal) extemporary
prayer (sometimes very passionate) is more usual.

Place and posture

Many Christians find it helpful to return to a familiar place
which they associate with prayer. This might be a church building;
it might be a favourite chair in a particular room. Some people use
visual or audio aids – music perhaps, or a cross, a candle, a picture,
an icon ...

Again, posture can be important. Some choose to kneel; others
prefer to sit in a comfortable chair. Many pray in bed. But prayer can
be offered anywhere: while walking or driving or ironing ... Many
Christians offer quick 'arrow prayers' throughout the day, and find
prayer a comfort if they cannot sleep at night.

Meditation and contemplation

Attention has been given by Christian writers on spirituality
to states of mind in prayer and methods of praying. *Meditation* and
contemplation are defined in various ways and contemplation is
often seen as a stage beyond meditation.

Meditation makes use of words and visual images.
Contemplation can dispense with both, though it may use a short
form of words, or a single word often repeated. Perhaps it is best
understood as a 'wordless' approach to God, which has no need of
the usual thought processes. Christian mystics down the centuries

have done their best to write about it, but have freely admitted that it defies adequate description.

> *So if you are to stand and not fall, never give up your firm intention: beat away at this cloud of unknowing between you and God with that sharp dart of longing love.*
>
> (from *The Cloud of Unknowing*, a fourteenth-century mystical work)

Christian worship

Christian worship is from God to God. Worship comes from God in two senses:
* it focuses on who God is and what he has done
* God himself puts into people's hearts and minds the desire for prayer and praise.

It is, of course, a human activity; but it is motivated, sustained and inspired by God himself. And so we can say truly that it is 'from God, to God'.

Because worship has this character, it can be seen as a kind of 'conversation' between God and the worshipping community. Through the reading of the Bible, the preaching of a sermon, the singing of psalms, canticles, songs and hymns, and in various other ways, God makes use of human words to speak to his people. He comforts and encourages us, he challenges and inspires us, and he calls us to particular acts of service.

Escapism?

Critics might argue that prayer and worship are an escape from 'the real world'. Christians would reply that it is necessary to withdraw from the world from time to time, in order to serve the world. Of course, not all acts of worship are inspiring and challenging. But some visionary writers have seen prayer and worship as nothing less than a bridge between heaven and earth.

Thomas Merton was one of the great spiritual writers of the twentieth century. In 1941 he visited an American monastery called Gethsemani, shortly before joining that community. It was a dark and troubled time in world history, especially in Europe where the Nazis were causing havoc. As he watched the monks at prayer, he came to see that activity as a focus of spiritual power. In his *Secular Journal* he wrote:

This is the center of America. I had wondered what was keeping the country together, what has been keeping the universe from cracking in pieces and falling apart. It's places like this monastery – not only this one; there must be others ... This is the only real city in America – and it is by itself, in the wilderness. It is an axle around which the whole country blindly turns, and knows nothing about it. Gethsemani holds the country together: What right have I to be here?

In Thomas Merton's view it was prayer – that mysterious and powerful means by which human beings are caught up in the plans and purposes of God – which holds the universe together and checks chaos.

Michael Ramsey (100th Archbishop of Canterbury) made the same point. He asserted that worship brings healing into a broken world, because it is a channel through which the love of God flows into our lives. He wrote about some of the great problems facing our world and continued with this 'parable':

A man had three nasty big boils, and he went to the doctor and asked for each of them to be treated or removed. And the doctor said 'I can do nothing permanent with these boils unless we get rid of the poison in your system which is causing them.' So, too, the human race, very sick and having at least three terrible boils in the social and moral order [great poverty, inequality, injustice ...], wants to be rid of them. But this human race does not grasp that the trouble is a poison in the system and the sickness is that of a deep derangement in the relation of mankind to the Creator. Go to the root. The root is the right relation of man to Creator: and when Christians are concerned about what they call worship they are concerned, not with something remote or escapist, but with the root of the world's predicament.

(*Introducing the Christian Faith*, SCM Press)

The sacraments

In times of conflict, a nation's flag assumes great significance. Indeed, people are sometimes willing to die rather than deny their national emblem. Viewed in one way, this is absurd. Who in their right mind would exchange life for a little bit of coloured cloth? But to those on the inside of that experience it is completely understandable. They see a 'little bit of coloured cloth', but they also see, represented in their flag, the past history of their nation and all that it stands for at its best. This notion of ordinary objects taking on deep significance is a helpful picture to hold in mind as we consider the sacraments of the Church.

When we call Christianity a 'sacramental religion', we refer to the fact that certain actions (eating, drinking, pouring) and physical objects (wine, bread, water) 'speak' powerfully of spiritual truths. This insight is found throughout the Hebrew Scriptures and in the Gospels. Later, the Church attempted various definitions. One of the most famous can be traced back to Augustine of Hippo: 'a sacrament is an outward and visible sign of an inward and spiritual grace'.

Christianity has two central sacraments: *Baptism* and *Holy Communion*. Both of these are representations of events in the life of Jesus Christ, but with a specific and personal significance for Christian worshippers today.

Who may be baptized?

Nobody is too old for baptism and all churches baptize adults who come to faith in Christ. But most churches baptize babies too, usually on the understanding that they will be given a Christian upbringing. These churches assert that infant baptism speaks clearly of the grace of God — indicating that his love is for all, even those who cannot consciously respond to it.

Holy communion

On the night before his crucifixion Jesus ate this meal with his disciples. When he broke the bread, he also broke with tradition, for he added the mysterious — and shocking — words, '*This is my body.*' He then took wine and added, '*This is my blood.*' As he gave the bread and wine to his disciples, he went on to say, '*Do this in remembrance of me.*' That instruction has been joyfully obeyed throughout the centuries. The Last Supper was to become the first of many, many more.

7

Christian faith in a scientific age

We live in an age in which many people assume two things:

First, that science has disproved religion.

Second, that to be a scientist is to disbelieve in God.

This chapter explores the reasons for these widely held views – from the persecution of Galileo, through the researches of Charles Darwin, to the fulminations of Richard Dawkins. It reveals that the actual situation is more complex, and more surprising, than is commonly assumed, as these words by Nobel prize-winning physicist Max Planck indicate:

'Religion and natural science are fighting a joint battle in an incessant never relaxing crusade against scepticism and against dogmatism, against disbelief and against superstition, and the rallying cry in this crusade has always been, and always will be: 'On to God'.

The origins of modern science

In a remarkable statement, the philosopher John Macmurray asserted that 'science is the legitimate child of a great religious movement, and its genealogy goes back to Jesus'. This is not to deny other important influences: Greek, Chinese, Egyptian, Arabian mathematics, the Old Testament (with its Wisdom literature and Creation narratives) ... But it is to affirm the importance for the rise of science as a widespread and particular way of looking at the universe, which Christianity gave to the Western world. Others have made the same point. For example, the philosopher A N Whitehead and the historian Herbert Butterfield both affirmed that science is a child of Christian thought.

So it comes as no surprise to learn that the prestigious Royal Society (founded by a gathering of leading British scientists in the seventeenth century) is dedicated 'to the Glory of God the Creator, and the benefit of the human race'. Two centuries later the British Association for the Advancement of Science held its first meeting in York. Those who gathered at that meeting in 1831 paid tribute to the Church, 'without whose aid the Association would never have been founded'. They went on to declare that 'true religion and true science ever lead to the same great end'. The Association's first two presidents were clergymen.

Several famous early scientists were devout Christians, some of whom wrote theological books as well as scientific works. Among many others we note: Isaac Newton (1642–1727), thought by many to be the greatest scientist of all time; Robert Boyle (1627–91), famous for Boyle's Law; Michael Faraday (1791–1867) who harnessed electro-magnetism; and Gregor Mendel (1822–84) who laid the groundwork for modern genetics while Abbot of a monastery. James Young Simpson (1811–70) was the first surgeon to employ the anaesthetic properties of chloroform. When asked to name his greatest discovery, his reported reply was, 'It is not chloroform. My greatest discovery has been to know that I am a sinner and that I could be saved by the grace of God.'

The present day

Professor Arnold Wolfendale, when appointed Astronomer Royal in 1991, declared, 'I think the hand of God can be seen everywhere'. This is not an isolated viewpoint, for many professional scientists believe in God and a number are convinced Christians. *Christians in Science* (formerly *The Research Scientists' Christian Fellowship*) has some 700 members in Britain; its American counterpart has about 2,000.

In Britain there is a flourishing Society for Ordained Scientists. Both Oxford and Cambridge universities have recently established centres to explore the interface between science and religion. Somewhat similar initiatives have been taken in the USA – at Berkeley, California and in Chicago, for example. Many believing scientists, including Professors Ian Barbour, John Lennox, Arthur Peacocke, John Polkinghorne and Russell Stannard, have written about the relationship between Christianity and science. (Paul Davies writes from a less orthodox standpoint.) From a very long list, we might also mention geneticists Professor 'Sam' Berry and Dr Francis Collins, the American who led the Human Genome Project for many years.

Professor Sir John Houghton is another eminent scientist who is a convinced Christian. A former Professor of Atmospheric Physics at Oxford University, he is an international figure in the vital field of climate change. On 7 December 2007 he was a member of the UN delegation which, alongside Al Gore, received the Nobel Peace Prize for outstanding work on global warming.

Of course, none of the above *proves* that Christianity is true. What it *does* show is that Christianity and science are not opposed. They are certainly not mutually exclusive.

If two teams really are in competition, no key player can be on both sides at the same time. And because scientists are intelligent people, the significant number of scientifically literate Christians also suggests that Christianity is not just a fairy story, suitable only for those who are unable to think for themselves.

The seeds of conflict

In view of all this, why has the notion that science has disproved religion become so widespread? We shall consider six reasons.

First, the notion of *purpose* lies outside scientific endeavour, by definition and choice, i.e. science is a deliberately 'self-limiting' activity. So science as an enterprise excludes the concept of God.

A second factor was the Galileo debate. **Galileo Galilei** (1564–1642) remained a Catholic throughout his life, but his harsh treatment at the hands of church officials is well known. Galileo built on the work of Copernicus (who was a canon in the church) in suggesting that the earth is not at the centre of the universe – an idea which was resisted by the church leadership of his day.

A third factor was the controversy over **Charles Darwin**'s research. His *Origin of Species by Means of Natural Selection* (1859) gave a very different account of the origins of life from that given in the Bible.

Charles Darwin himself was not an opponent of Christianity. It is true that he gradually lost his faith (partly through the death of his young daughter, Annie). But in 1872 (13 years after the *Origin of Species*) he gladly accepted honorary membership of the Anglican South American Missionary Society, because he was so impressed with their work. In reply to their invitation, he wrote, 'I shall feel proud if your committee think fit to elect me an honorary member of your society.' 'SAMS' continues to do excellent work today.

A fourth factor relates to the above. Some modern fundamentalist Christians are keen to keep the Darwinian controversy alive. They assert that evolution is a discredited theory and that the chapters on Creation in Genesis should be read literally.

A fifth factor arises from the work of **Sigmund Freud** (1856–1939) who made an immense impact upon the way we view the world.

Freud has given us a new vocabulary (unconscious, ego, id, superego, Oedipus complex, Freudian slip) and a new understanding of ourselves. Freud maintained that he was making a *scientific* analysis of human behaviour – a view contested by many, including non-Christians.

He wrote about religion and asserted that a key Christian insight should be inverted. God has not made us in his image; rather, we have made God in our image – according to our deepest needs.

Carl Gustav Jung, another of the founders of modern psychology, was much more sympathetic to religion. He made the following remarkable statement:

> *During the past 30 years people from all the civilized countries of the earth have consulted me ... Among my patients in the second half of life – that is to say over 35 – there has not been one whose problem in the last resort was not that of finding a religious outlook on life.*

Finally we note the hostility or indifference towards religion of some articulate present-day exponents of science. As we have seen, many scientists are practising Christians. But some non-Christian scientists have captured the popular imagination. Richard Dawkins with *The Selfish Gene* and his bestseller *The God Delusion* is the best known. Such aggressively atheistic scientists may appear to be speaking 'on behalf of science'; in fact, they are private individuals, whose views on religion are opposed by many of their fellow scientists. Significantly, despite its huge popularity, *The God Delusion* received some bad reviews from both atheists and scientists for its belligerent 'atheistic fundamentalism'.

Resolving the tension: 'complementarity'

'Reductionism' refers to the process of 'reducing' complex areas of life to a simple one-level explanation. Notable among such explanations is Professor C E M Joad's description of human beings.

'Man is nothing but:
* FAT enough for seven bars of soap
* LIME enough to whitewash one chicken coop
* PHOSPHORUS enough to tip 2200 matches

* IRON enough for one medium-sized nail
* MAGNESIUM enough for one dose of salts
* POTASH enough to explode one toy crane
* SUGAR enough for seven cups of tea
* SULPHUR enough to rid one dog of fleas.'

In this tongue-in-cheek description, Professor Joad (who came to embrace the Christian faith in later life) provides a classic example of *reductionism*. The flaw is in the phrase 'nothing but'. His description gives a perfectly legitimate description of a human being. But it is not complete; other kinds and levels of description are required.

We need to add *psychological* categories, for human beings have emotions and ideas. We will wish to add *sociological* categories, for human beings function in communities. And these descriptions do not rule out the possibility of *spiritual* categories, for human beings experience love and have an instinct for worship. These various levels of description and explanation are 'complementary': each adds to the others and together they give a fuller and more accurate account.

This approach applies to everything. Music *is* vibrations in the air and ink dots on paper (even cat-gut or steel on horse hair, if we are listening to a cello). But it is not *just* these things. Ask the audience. And we are bound to ask how it is that music and art have the power to inspire and disturb us. The same approach is true when we consider the universe itself. We might describe it in terms of its origins in 'the big bang' some 14,000 million years ago. But this explanation, which uses the categories of modern physics, does not rule out the possibility of explaining the universe as the creation of a God of love.

Why does the earth support life? An answer in *scientific* terms will discuss factors like the importance of carbon, the immensity of space, the size of the earth (just right to support an atmosphere) and the theory of evolution. But it is equally possible to give an explanation in *theological* terms – by maintaining that God designed the earth so that these factors apply. If this is the case, then scientists are discovering the way in which God has designed the world – 'thinking God's thoughts after him' as the early astronomer Johannes Kepler put it. Science itself can help us to see the grandeur of God.

Of course, this theological explanation may be untrue. But not *because* of the fact that Nature can be explained in scientific terms.

Resolving the tension: facts and faith

In a recent radio discussion, a member of the panel asserted that science is about facts, and religion is about faith. Now of course all religions involve faith. But they include facts too. This is certainly true of Christianity which, like science, is based on *interpreted facts*. One fact is the Bible's account of Jesus of Nazareth which is very difficult to explain in other than Christian terms. Another fact is the rise of the Christian movement in apparently impossible circumstances (with a shrinking number of demoralized disciples and an executed leader). And so we could go on. There are plenty of facts; and faith builds on these.

Conversely, there is plenty of *faith* in science. Scientific method can be described as observation, hypothesis and experimentation, leading to inference and theory. But it can equally well be described in terms of hunch, intuition, gamble, accident, teamwork, flashes of insight, patient slog, with plenty of faith mixed in; and numerous conversations over coffee and beer! Both sets of factors are present all the time. The great Albert Einstein asserted that '*God does not play dice.*' And his statement of faith, that there is a constancy and reality about nature, is fundamental to the scientific enterprise.

Ethical dilemmas

Science has given the world many blessings. Most of us would not wish to live in a world without anaesthetics, without television and without toothpaste. But science has presented us with enormous problems too. The possible destruction of our planet, whether by nuclear explosion or global warming, is not just the stuff of science fiction. Some commentators are very pessimistic. David Bosch wrote:

It is becoming increasingly evident that the modern gods of the West – science, technology and industrialization – have lost their magic. Events of world history have shaken Western civilization to the core ... we are heading for an ecological disaster on a cosmic scale ... progress was, in effect, a false god.

Medical science, too, presents us with great problems as well as numerous blessings. To take just one example: we now have the ability to discern early in pregnancy whether a baby is likely to have certain grave health problems and whether it will be male or female. This means that we also have the ability to decide which babies will actually be born. With such knowledge comes a threat to the gender balance – already a practical concern in some societies today.

Numerous new ethical and practical decisions press in upon us in the early decades of the twenty-first century. Scientists themselves do not wish to carry the burden of decision-making on their own. This is a task for all of us. It is a task which Christians, together with many others, take very seriously. We believe that prayer and a study of the wisdom to be found in previous generations – especially in the ancient Scriptures – have a practical part to play in seeking to ensure that science enriches, and does not destroy, life on planet Earth. In particular, the biblical teaching that God has given us stewardship of our world, is a vital insight. Nature is not a treasure-trove to be ransacked; it is a delicate network to be respected, cherished and left in good order for future generations.

Science ... does not deal in certainties. The best it can do is convince us, on the basis of strong probabilities – and that depends on trust.

(Professor Lisa Jardine)

'It is indeed a sobering thought that the early writings of the Jewish people (i.e. our Old Testament) encompass all the basic recommendations of world conservation strategy.'

(Professor David Bellamy)

Natural allies?

The above quotation from botanist David Bellamy indicates that some scientists view religious faith and scientific endeavour as natural – perhaps essential – allies. The following statements show that this belief is not uncommon.

The more I examine the universe and the details of its architecture, the more evidence I find that the universe in some sense must have known we were coming.

(Freeman Dyson, theoretical physicist)

Science brings man nearer to God.

(Louis Pasteur, who revolutionized microbiology and gave his name to pasteurized milk)

Historically, religion came first and science grew out of religion. Science has never superseded religion, and it is my expectation that it never will supersede it.

(Arnold Toynbee, historian)

Scientists have discovered that the laws of nature have to be 'finely-tuned' to allow the possibility for life to develop. If the power of gravity, or the charge on the electron, or the nature of nuclear forces, were even a little different from what they actually are, no life could have come into being ... Life is not possible in 'any old world'; it requires a universe in a trillion.

(John Polkinghorne, mathematical physicist)

I'm not an atheist. We are in the position of a little child entering a huge library filled with books in many different languages. The child knows someone must have written those books. It does not know how. The child dimly suspects a mysterious order in the arrangement of the books but doesn't know what it is. That, it seems to me, is the attitude of even the most intelligent human being toward God.

(Albert Einstein)

One Church, many churches

Many people in the West have little contact with the Church. Fed by the media, they believe that most churches are empty and unwelcoming, and that Christian worship is lacking in joy or relevance. No doubt such churches do exist. But it's easy to find, even in modern Britain, large congregations and inspiring worship. There are still more people in churches at the weekend than in football stadiums.

Move out of secular, superstitious Europe and the Church worldwide is growing fast. And in some unlikely places too – China, for example.

The Christian Church remains the largest movement in all history – by a long way. This isn't stated in a spirit of competitive superiority; it is simply a statement of significant fact.

This is important background as we consider the worldwide Christian Church. In this chapter we'll explore the history and rich diversity of the world's many churches, all of which seek to worship God and to express a living faith in Jesus Christ by serving our divided and troubled world.

The Christian Church is like a great mountain. If we stand looking at it, and even if we are on it, we cannot see all sides at the same time. The view from another vantage point may be very different from ours. The aim of this chapter is to walk round and up the mountain to gain a fuller impression of the whole; an institution, a community of peoples and a vital factor in any view of world history.

If it is One Church, one mountain, why are there so many different churches? All Christians, whatever their race or status, are united 'in Christ' – in his love, grace and forgiveness. So there can only be One Church, one body of Christians, spread through all generations and throughout the world (for which the Greek word is 'Katholikos'). Hence the phrase in the Nicene Creed – an important ancient summary of belief – 'We believe in one holy, *catholic* and apostolic Church.'

As the centuries wore on, Christianity spread through all the nations of the known world and its detailed beliefs and practices were hammered out. Different opinions and claims about authenticity and authority caused some groups of Christians to separate from others. At times they even fought and persecuted each other. One encouraging feature of the twentieth century was that Christians with a different history and tradition recognized each other again. They came together in discussion, in mutual agreement and, in some cases, in visible reunion.

But great Christian 'blocs' remain and in this chapter we shall outline the main distinctive features of:

* the Roman Catholic Church with 1,143 million members (including some 6 million Catholic Christians who do not owe allegiance to Rome)
* Protestant Churches with 277 million members
* the various Orthodox Churches with 220 million members
* Independent Churches with 438 million members
* Anglican Churches with 83 million members

Across these various denominational groups are spread the many Christians who belong to different Pentecostal or Charismatic churches or groups. In addition there are about 35 million members of groups that claim to be Christian but which are outside mainstream Christianity (such as Jehovah's Witnesses, Mormons, Christian Scientists, Unitarians, Spiritualists and British Israelites).

The Orthodox Churches

We start with those Churches which have preserved ancient structures and forms most tenaciously throughout the centuries. These are the Churches of Eastern Europe: the Greek, Balkan and Russian 'Orthodox Churches'. 'Orthodox' means right teaching. These Churches maintain they have kept the apostolic faith most faithfully, while alleging that Catholics and Protestants have diverged from it – by adding what is new or non-genuine, or subtracting what is original and authentic.

To go into an Eastern Orthodox church is like stepping back a thousand years or more; neither the furnishings nor the ritual seem to have changed at all. Often the building itself is centuries old and crumbling, with clouds of incense surrounding the worshippers. Religious paintings (icons) are placed around the church. They are surrounded by candles, with people bowing in reverence in front of them and kissing them. Behind an elaborate screen (the *iconostasis*) priests and deacons move about in glorious vestments, engaged in ancient ceremony.

And a small choir, often at the western end, raises you to heaven with the rise and fall of persistent chanting, in Greek or Old Church Slavonic, with the deepest of bass voices you have ever heard coming through to shiver your timbers in ecstasy. Often there are no pews; just seats around the edge for the infirm (as in medieval churches; hence the phrase 'the weakest to the wall').

To be a faithful Orthodox Christian you should attend the liturgy, pray to God, Jesus, Mary and the saints, and heed your parish priest. The parish priest is usually a married man of local origin. He is likely to remain in his village all his life; in this too he is much like his flock. In general, learning belongs not to the parish clergy but to the monasteries, where celibacy, poverty and total obedience to superiors are required. All bishops come from the monasteries, although there is a long tradition of lay theologians – highly educated lay people who are teachers and writers. A number of Orthodox congregations – often small, but usually growing – have established themselves in Britain and the USA.

The Roman Catholic Church

To be a Roman Catholic is to be conscious of belonging to a Church of immense size and global spread, which claims to be the nearest to the sort of Church that Christ wants. It is also to be part of a long tradition of colourful worship and deep spirituality. Worship styles vary despite the rigid outward structures.

The Roman Catholic Church has often been able to tolerate and live with local customs, religions and beliefs to such a degree that some other Christians accuse it of compromise – even of encouraging pagan practice and superstition. But Pope John Paul II spoke out against astrology and horoscopes as being incompatible with Christian faith. Even so, they remain popular throughout the Western world, including Italy.

The *monastic movement* has always played a significant role in Roman Catholicism. At their best, monasteries have been powerhouses of prayer, worship and evangelization, and centres for experimental change. Because the vast majority of parish priests are required to be celibate, the distinction between monks and parish priests is not so obvious as in the Eastern Churches.

Whether clergy should be celibate is keenly debated within the Roman Catholic Church. Some of its members believe that papal insistence on this is one cause of an alarming fall in vocations to the priesthood. At the same time, many priests are not allowed to exercise their priesthood, because they have married after ordination. One estimate puts this figure as high as one-fifth of the total number of priests worldwide. (*Note: There are some married Roman Catholic priests but they are the exception e.g. some married Anglican priests, who left the Church of England because of the ordination of women priests, were later ordained as priests in the Roman Catholic Church.*)

Protestant Churches

In the sixteenth century there was turmoil in Europe. The Reformation – a movement for reform within the Medieval Church – was the inspiration and ultimate cause of most Churches other than Orthodox or Catholic. The Reformation resulted partly from the rediscovery of the ancient languages of Hebrew and Greek, which meant that the Scriptures could be read in the original. For the previous 12 centuries, the Latin tradition had totally dominated the West. A second cause of the Reformation was the growing nationalism in various European countries; this led to a desire for freedom from the influence and power of Rome. A further cause was reaction to the abuses which developed in the Catholic Church, during the latter decades of the Middle Ages.

The Reformation could have resulted in reforms in teaching and practice *within* the Catholic Church, had it not met total resistance from the central authority in Rome. All attempts at reconciliation failed and new church groupings emerged. Each of these protested at the claims and power of Rome, hence 'Protestant' Churches. (The term was first used at the Diet of Speyer in 1529.) These Churches emphasized different elements in the practices and beliefs of the Church before it was corrupted (as they saw it) by Rome. Because of this, and since they emerged in different countries at a time when nationalism was so strong, they fell into four main groups: Lutheran; Reformed (or Presbyterian); Baptist; Anglican.

In later centuries they were joined by two other 'breakaway' Churches: Methodist (eighteenth century) and Pentecostal (twentieth century). All Protestant churches placed great emphasis on the Bible as the controlling authority for belief and practice. They wished to make the Scriptures readily available and easy to read. And they wanted to simplify worship, so that important elements would stand out and not be overwhelmed by trivial or misleading ceremonies, or by ornate music. They emphasized the importance of preaching alongside, or above, the administration of the sacraments. Many churches in the sixteenth century (including the

Church of England) substituted the authority of the local monarch for that of the Pope in Rome.

Pentecostal Churches

Pentecostalists take their name from Acts 2, where God's Spirit came in power on Peter and the other disciples ('the Feast of Pentecost'). God's Spirit enabled the disciples to go out with zeal to spread the gospel, and gave them miraculous powers to speak in 'other tongues' and to heal the sick.

Pentecostal Christians believe that such powers are still available today, through the Holy Spirit. Pentecostal churches were established early in the twentieth century and are growing fast throughout the world today. Their worship is informal, exuberant and partly unplanned, because of their belief in the immediacy of the gifts of the Spirit. The word 'charismatic' is often used for this expression of Christianity, but charismatic worship of an exuberant kind is found in the older 'mainstream' churches too.

Independent Churches

Independent Churches (indigenous or locally founded churches) are springing up around the world. Some African and Asian churches have arisen partly in adverse reaction to the Western elements which inevitably became associated with the missionary work of previous centuries. They are strong numerically but diverse in character. Often they are Pentecostal in emphasis but some stress the practices (and sometimes also the teachings and culture) of their countries before the missionaries arrived. Throughout the world, Independent, Pentecostal and Charismatic churches are growing faster than any other tradition. Taken together, they number about 438 million, although their independent character makes them difficult to enumerate.

Older independent churches, for example, Seventh Day Adventists, Moravians, Mennonites and Nazerenes, have long been an important part of the Christian landscape.

A shifting centre of gravity

Christianity started in the Middle East and was found very early in North Africa (see Acts 8:27). But throughout most of its history Europe has taken the lead, dominating both its thinking and its expansion – although the USA took over this leadership role during the twentieth century.

The eighteenth, nineteenth and early twentieth centuries saw a remarkable burst of missionary zeal. Britain, the USA and other countries sent missionaries to the four corners of the earth. As a result, the Christian Church has been planted in every continent and in almost every country. Christianity has shown itself capable of adapting to all cultures. In every society there are customs which need to be challenged in the name of Christ. But in every place, aspects of local custom and culture are found to be effective vehicles for Christian teaching and worship. Today, it is the relatively young churches which are flourishing. So the Christian Church worldwide is growing and the Christian faith continues to spread. Meanwhile, the Church's centre of gravity has shifted:

* *from* Europe and (to a lesser extent) the USA
* *to* Africa, Asia, and Latin America.

Conclusion

At the beginning of this chapter, the image of a mountain was used to illustrate the one Church in its different aspects. Another image is the river which flows from one single spring. The spring is Jesus Christ himself, who gives 'living water' (John 4:10). All the water flows from the same source, but it forms many streams. Separate as we are, we acknowledge that the living water matters more than any particular river.

Church
and
Society

From the outset, Christians knew that if their faith was to be true to the teaching of Jesus, it must impact on their personal lifestyle – and on society. Before long they made themselves popular by organizing feeding programmes for thousands of hungry people in Rome. And they made themselves *unpopular* by opposing some commonly accepted practices e.g. killing unwanted babies by exposure.

Since then, Christians have founded schools, universities, hospitals and hospices as well as famous organizations such as Amnesty, Barnardos, Save the Children, Samaritans, Shelter, and the Hospice movement.

William Wilberforce led fellow believers – and others – in the long fight to abolish slavery. And two centuries later Martin Luther King, a Baptist pastor, led the civil rights movement in the USA.

From the earliest days the Church has needed to work out its position in relation to society. At first it was a minority group, often persecuted. The small but growing band of disciples developed a distinctive lifestyle based on love for God and neighbour, and witness to their risen Lord, within a suspicious and hostile society. They recalled the vivid images used by Jesus; they were to be 'salt', 'light' and 'peacemakers' within their communities.

A radical change took place when the Emperor Constantine embraced the Christian faith in AD 312. No longer outlawed or marginalized, Christians had to learn how to wield secular power. There were attempts to turn back the clock. The pagan Emperor Julian ('the Apostate', c. 331–363) wished his subjects to honour his gods and worked hard to bring this about. He failed, and paid a moving tribute to the power of Christian love. It is a clear example of the Christian faith at its best, making an impact on society. Julian referred to Christian believers as 'atheists' and 'godless Galileans', for they worshipped one invisible God and denied his gods:

Atheism [i.e. Christian faith] has been specially advanced through the loving service rendered to strangers, and through their care for the burial of the dead. It is a scandal that there is not a single Jew who is a beggar, and that the godless Galileans care not only for their own poor but for ours as well; while those who belong to us look in vain for the help that we should render them.

Power and persecution

Jesus came 'not to be served but to serve'. At the Last Supper he washed his disciples' feet as an example of humble service (John 13:15). But the Church has not always stayed close to its Founder's intentions. In its strength the Church has often betrayed its Lord. This is partly due to the fact that Christians share the prejudices and many of the assumptions found in every culture and period of history. It has also resulted from corruption within the Church. Men far from the Spirit of Christ, and with little regard for the teaching of Christ, nevertheless found positions of power within the Church of Christ. As a result, the impact of the Church on Society has sometimes been harmful.

But the Church itself has been subject to tyranny over the centuries. In the twentieth century, the Church in Europe found itself in the shadow of two especially hostile ideologies.

Nazism

Like many others, Church leaders found it difficult to see the shape of things to come, when Hitler took power. Within the Roman Catholic Church, leadership was sometimes weak and uncertain. But some bishops and priests stood firm and several were martyred. The Catholic dean of the cathedral in Berlin protested from his pulpit against the persecution of Jews; he died on the way to a concentration camp. Opposition by Church leaders caused Hitler to drop his 'euthanasia for incurables' plan. And '*Pope Pius XII secretly allowed himself to be used as a channel of communication between the German conspirators against Hitler and the British government*' (Professor Owen Chadwick).

Among German Protestants, the Confessing Church opposed the Nazi regime. Lutheran pastor Martin Niemöller was a leading member who was imprisoned in a concentration camp by Hitler in 1937. He refused offers of conditional release and stayed there until 1945. Dietrich Bonhoeffer was another important figure. Tragically, he was executed by the Nazis just before the end of the war.

Communism

Following the Russian Revolution of 1917 the Church came under an atheist dictatorship. Some 8,000 priests and nuns were assassinated during Lenin's lifetime. Under Stalin (1879–1953) it was difficult for Christians in the USSR even to meet for worship.

Christian initiatives

The impact upon society of Christian individuals and groups continued into the twentieth century. Christian Socialists like Archbishop William Temple helped prepare for Britain's Welfare State and many modern caring agencies have Christian origins.

Samaritans was started by an Anglican rector in London. Chad Varah became aware that a large number of people were in despair and suicidal. He invited them to ring Mansion House 9000. Within 20 years this telephone ministry of listening and befriending had grown into an international movement.

Shelter is an influential pressure group for good housing in Britain. It began on 1 December 1966 as the result of the united concern of five housing organizations, three of which contained the word Catholic, Christian or Church. Christian leaders were key figures in those early days and Shelter's first chairman, Bruce Kenrick, was a Christian minister.

Habitat for Humanity is an American initiative which builds subsidized homes for needy families in the USA. It has also pioneered 'appropriate technology' homes in other continents and countries (Tanzania, for example).

The Hospice Movement was started in Britain under the inspiration of Dame Cicely Saunders. She pioneered pain control and saw the need for small, intimate units, where terminally ill patients could be cared for and families and friends welcomed. Dame Cicely gladly acknowledged that without the inspiration and power of Jesus Christ, she would have lacked the strength needed to establish the movement. Her vision and practical ideas caught on and hospices are now found around the world.

Amnesty International was founded by Peter Benenson, a Christian lawyer. Concerned at the plight of prisoners of conscience, he prayed in the crypt of St Martin-in-the-Fields in London's Trafalgar Square. He developed the idea of a network of people who would write to, and about, prisoners of conscience, and speak on their behalf. At a practical level, the existing network of churches was important. Peter Benenson launched the movement on Trinity Sunday 1961 to emphasize 'that the power of the Holy Spirit works to bring together people of diverse origins by influencing their common conscience'.

When the first 200 letters came, the guards gave me back my clothes. When the next 200 letters came, the prison Director came to see me. When the next pile of letters arrived, the Director got in touch with his superior. The letters kept arriving,

and the President was informed. The letters still kept arriving,
and the President called the prison and told them to let me go.

(From a letter by a former prisoner of conscience)

These movements are not limited to Christian believers.
In most cases a wide range of views and beliefs are to be found
among their activists. It remains true that these organizations were
built on Christian foundations, with Christian vision and energy.

A focus for dissent

The Church has often been a natural focus for dissent against
established authority. In the twentieth century this was extremely
important in many places and for many issues.

Martin Luther King (1929–68)

By personal charisma, courage, brilliant organization and
moving rhetoric, Martin Luther King – Pastor of Ebenezer Baptist
Church in Atlanta – led a massive non-violent movement in
an attempt to establish equality for black citizens in the USA.
Like Gandhi, upon whom he based his campaign of non-violent
resistance, Dr King was assassinated.

The Berlin Wall

As Marxism came to a swift end throughout Europe in
the late 1980s, the Christian churches were a natural rallying
point for dissent from the old order. Large prayer vigils were
held, with flickering candles, communal singing and inspiring
addresses. The churches in Eastern Europe are finding life in the
new order easier (in that they are no longer persecuted) but more
complex. Materialism, commercialism and hedonism may yet
prove more corrosive than Marxism. Some Eastern Europeans look
back to the old order with nostalgia.

South Africa

The old white-dominated order in South Africa claimed to be
Christian, and the ruling white party was closely linked with the
Dutch Reformed Church. But dissent often found expression in the

churches. Best known among black Christian leaders is Desmond Tutu (Nobel Peace Prize winner), but there are many others.

The new democratic South Africa is, thus far, a 'success' story, but there is a long road to travel and levels of violence – a legacy from the days of apartheid – are still extremely high. In his autobiography (*Long Walk to Freedom*) Nelson Mandela is not uncritical of the churches, especially the Dutch Reformed Church. But he speaks affectionately of the church of his childhood: '... *the Church was as concerned with this world as the next: I saw that virtually all of the achievements of Africans seemed to have come about through the missionary work of the Church*'. He pays special tribute to his black Methodist housemaster (the Revd S S Mokitimi) and to Archbishops Trevor Huddleston and Desmond Tutu.

Failure

As with all human endeavours, we find the bad alongside the good.

One shameful area of failure and disgrace is that of child abuse. A number of priests have been accused of this and some have been found guilty. Church leaders have been accused of a 'cover-up'. This appalling scandal continues to rock the worldwide Catholic Church.

Current issues

The Churches have been energetic in thinking and acting on a wide range of issues. At international and national levels the Churches have eminent Christian specialists, with a wide range of expertise, upon whom they can call. But concern is also shown at the local level. For example, several Roman Catholic churches have a 'justice and peace' group. And in many British cities and towns Christians have practical schemes to help homeless people (e.g. Nightstop UK for vulnerable young people).

An issue often in the news – and sometimes in the law courts – is whether the Christian faith any longer has a public role, or whether it should be confined to the sphere of private preference. Advocates for public influence point out that European law and custom is based on Judeo-Christian ethics, including the Ten Commandments. Opponents urge that this is no longer relevant in a secular society.

One world, many faiths

> Today Britain is home to many faiths, but I hope it doesn't lose its own — the Christian faith that inspired its greatest poetry, its finest architecture, and its bravest battles in defence of freedom.
>
> (Chief Rabbi, Sir Jonathan Sacks)

In relation to Britain's population (60 million and rising – and ageing), the number of adherents of non-Christian faiths is relatively small. Some towns and cities have many temples, gurdwaras, synagogues and mosques to cater for Hindus, Sikhs, Jews, Muslims and others. The total number following faiths other than Christianity in Britain is about 8 per cent – a figure that is growing. Some Christians are keenly aware of the need to understand other faiths and to communicate across cultural and religious boundaries. The need for dialogue between the great faiths is seen as even more pressing in the light of the events of 11 September 2001 and 7 July 2005.

Perhaps, in the end, only one thing is more important for the future of our world than inter-faith dialogue. And that is inter-faith friendship.

Archbishop Rowan Williams sets before us a Christian approach that marries confidence in the gospel with humility towards those who hold a different viewpoint, or believe a different creed:

> 'There is a confidence that arises from being utterly convinced that the Christian creed and the Christian vision have in them a life and a richness that can embrace and transfigure all the complexities of human life. This confidence can rightly sit alongside a patient willingness to learn from others in the ordinary encounters of life together in our varied society.'

10

a great inheritance

Christianity has made an immense impact on our culture and landscape. Much of our greatest music, art, architecture and literature was – and is – inspired by Christian themes.

Whether we consider Bach's *St Matthew Passion* or the influence of Gospel music on Elvis Presley; the poetry of T S Eliot or the novels of Graham Greene, Christian impact is inescapable.

The European countryside – as elsewhere, including the Americas – is beautified by thousands of church buildings, from immense cathedrals to tiny exquisite churches.

But our greatest inheritance is from the men and women who have handed on the torch of personal faith down the generations.

The earliest days

Jesus' ministry took place mainly in the open air. Neither his little group of followers, nor the crowds who flocked to hear him, required a building or needed any visual magnificence. From time to time this has also been true for later Christians, and a meeting for worship in the open air – perhaps in a garden or beside a lake – is often a treasured memory. But this does not mean that Jesus rejected all holy places and buildings, or their splendid decoration. Indeed, after his resurrection his first disciples met daily in the Temple precincts.

But Christianity quickly separated from its Jewish roots. The early believers soon realized that Jesus' life, death and resurrection had made both Temple and animal sacrifices redundant. The early Christians came to see that on the cross, Jesus had become our Great High Priest, who had offered the one perfect sacrifice for sin: his own life.

At first, Christian worship took place in people's homes or in the open air. That did not last long. Any movement which passes into a second and third generation tends to become an institution. This happened to the Church. As it increased in numbers and spread through different countries and cultures, it developed an organization with identifiable 'places'.

The best known early places are the *catacombs* (burial chambers), where people could meet underground for worship and to commemorate their dead. This invisible meeting place was ideal, for the Church was intermittently persecuted for the first 300 years. As soon as specific places became identified with Christianity, art was employed to beautify and to instruct. The catacomb paintings are the earliest known form of Christian art. They often show Jesus as:

* the Good Shepherd
* the King who promises salvation
* the giver of the Communion meal.

Not all Christian worship had to be secretive, even during the first 300 years. The earliest known Christian church is a house adapted soon after AD 200, in Dura Europos in Syria. Two rooms

were turned into a baptistry and decorated with wall paintings.
A similar house church, from two centuries later, has been found in
Britain at Lullingstone in Kent.

The holiest and the grandest

As soon as the public building of churches was possible,
a longing to locate the sites of central events in Jesus' ministry
made itself felt. The most holy place in all Christendom is the
Church of the Holy Sepulchre in Jerusalem. This vast building
stands over the place where Jesus was crucified – and where his
tomb was located, according to fourth-century Christians
(a claim which has been supported by recent archaeology). Around
the remains of the rock tomb of Jesus, there still stands a huge
octagonal shape built by Constantine the Great in the fourth
century. He also built a basilica over the site of the Nativity in
Bethlehem. The great church now standing there, over the cave
celebrated as Jesus' birthplace, dates from the next century.
(Caves were, and are, used as stables.)

The most memorable churches are grand buildings in cities and
towns, built under the patronage of a king, bishop or other wealthy
person. But most churches were humble buildings in villages. The
vast majority were of timber, built in the same way as huts and
barns. Few have survived from earlier than the thirteenth century.
The earliest in Europe is in Greensted, Essex, dating from the
eleventh century. There are twenty or so stave (timber) churches in
Norway which survive from the twelfth century onwards.

Decoration

A wide range of visual arts was employed. Carvings in stone
became a feature of Christian decoration from the beginning. These
often depicted scenes from the Bible and the lives of saints. Carvings
in wood were also made but fewer have survived, since wood is more
vulnerable than stone. Work in textiles (including embroidery), gold,
silver and jewellery was also commissioned by the Christian Church.
The clothes worn by the ministers – and the carpets, draperies and

other furnishings – should be, it was felt, the finest possible. Altar frontals, episcopal and priestly vestments, and the vessels for use in the celebration of the Eucharist became very fine – at least the equal of any to be seen in the palaces of kings and emperors.

Monasteries became centres for the production of books – many of them beautifully scripted and illustrated. The *Lindisfarne Gospels* were made on Holy Island (Lindisfarne) in Northumbria around 700, 'in honour of St Cuthbert'. In 950, a priest called Aldred wrote an Anglo-Saxon translation between the lines of the Latin text.

From the early days in the catacombs, Christians expressed their faith through paintings. In the East this took a unique form – the icon – which has recently become known, admired and copied in the West and worldwide. An icon is a stylized painting on wood of a Christian subject, usually Christ or a saint. Icons are painted according to strict rules which are devotional as well as artistic.

Glory to God in the highest

In one sense Christianity has no holy places. Unlike a Muslim or a Hindu, a Christian is under no obligation to make a pilgrimage. God can be experienced with equal power and worshipped with equal validity in every place.

But it is a universal human need, which Christianity in no way denies, that people need a place, usually a building, which is set apart (which is what the word 'holy' means) for the worship of the Creator and Sustainer of the universe. These places remind us of the claims upon us of that which is greater than ourselves. In building and decorating such places, we offer our skills, our labour and our most precious gifts as tokens of our worship. For, as the Bible makes abundantly clear, true worship involves nothing less than the offering of our lives to be 'a living sacrifice' (Romans 12:1–2).

Magnificent music to wonderful words

The decades from 1600 onwards saw a magnificent flowering of church music, notably in Italy, and the beginnings of oratorio.

But it was the Lutheran J S Bach (1685–1750) who emerged as possibly the greatest composer ever produced by Western culture. As an organist he was breathtaking, as a composer, prolific. He set Bible narrative to music as none before or since. His contemporary G F Handel wrote many oratorios, including *Messiah* (1741) – possibly the most popular of all religious compositions. This work retains its wide appeal, and has given rise to many choirs formed to sing it. Haydn's *The Creation* (composed in 1798) is another great work from the oratorio repertoire by a devout Christian.

Haydn, Schubert, Verdi and Brahms are among a number of first-rank composers who wrote a Mass (sometimes more than one). This is a musical setting to five lyrical and significant passages from the Latin service. Among the greatest are Mozart's *Requiem Mass* (1791), Bach's *Mass in B Minor* (completed in 1738), and Beethoven's *Mass in D* (1825).

Many of today's composers – such as John Rutter, John Tavener, James MacMillan, Andrew Carter, Malcolm Archer, Philip Moore, Bob Chilcott and Richard Shephard – find inspiration from Christian themes.

The literature of faith

Caedmon (seventh century) is the earliest known English Christian poet; he is credited with the earliest surviving Christian hymn in the English language. The prose of King Alfred (848–99), like much of the whole corpus of Old and Middle English, clearly comes within the same tradition of faith.

The Mystery Plays of the thirteenth to sixteenth centuries have enjoyed a new lease of life in our own day. Following the Miracle Plays, they probably took their name from the 'mysteries' or trade guilds who performed them. They vividly presented great Bible events from the Creation onwards, developing strong local styles and texts, especially in the north of England.

The writing of Geoffrey Chaucer (*c.* 1342–1400), together with his near contemporary William Langland and his successors, Spenser, Shakespeare and other Elizabethans, reflect their Christian heritage. Two masters of English prose who paid for their writings with their lives were the liturgical reformer Thomas Cranmer, and the Bible translator William Tyndale. The former enabled English speakers to pray in their own tongue; the latter made it possible for them to read or hear the Scriptures in English. We have already noted Melvyn Bragg's astonishing statement that Tyndale's work is 'probably the most influential book that's ever been in the history of language – English or any other'.

The poet George Herbert (1593–1633) and the satirist Jonathan Swift (1667–1745) were clergymen and Samuel Johnson (1709–84) was a devout layman. John Donne, appointed Dean of St Paul's Cathedral in 1621, is remembered for both religious and erotic poetry and for his powerful and original sermons.

> *... No man is an island, entire of itself. Every man is a piece of the continent, a part of the main. If a clod be washed away by the sea, Europe is the less, as well as if a promontory were, as well as if a manor of thy friends or of thine own were. Any man's death diminishes me, because I am involved with mankind. And therefore never send to know for whom the bell tolls; it tolls for thee.*

(John Donne, *Devotions upon Emergent Occasions*)

Two other Johns, Milton (1608–74) and Bunyan (1628–88), the scholar-statesman and the tinker-preacher, both stand in the Puritan tradition. Each produced several works of enduring worth and one masterpiece; in order, *Paradise Lost* and *Pilgrim's Progress*. Both created unforgettable images in verse and prose respectively, one from his study, the other largely from a prison cell. Each used his powerful imagination to illuminate eternal truth and practical living, from the enticement of temptation in the garden of Eden to the trials and triumphs of Christian pilgrims in this world's Vanity Fair.

Among the more committed but less predictable authors was William Blake (1757–1827), visionary poet, painter and engraver. His poem 'Jerusalem' has become a popular and rousing hymn. Blake is one of those who would be surprised to find their prophetic verses adopted and domesticated in this way.

To the present day

Many nineteenth-century poets explored questions of religious faith and doubt, including Samuel Taylor Coleridge, William Wordsworth, Robert Browning, Lord Alfred Tennyson and Matthew Arnold. Among twentieth-century Christian poets we note T S Eliot (a key figure in the transformation of poetry), Gerard Manley Hopkins (undiscovered until the twentieth century), Jack Clemo, Norman Nicholson, R S Thomas and W H Auden. David Adam and others have popularized a revived Celtic culture. *The river wanders, varies in pace and depth, but never runs dry*.

The desire to explore and explain the Christian faith prompted apologetics (the defence of the faith), novels, poetry, essays and drama from twentieth-century believers such as Dorothy L Sayers, C S Lewis, G K Chesterton, J R R Tolkien and Charles Williams. Three Catholic writers – Anthony Burgess, Graham Greene and Evelyn Waugh – were powerful novelists, whose religious background and troubled faith strongly influenced their work. Novels and plays by Christians and unbelievers continue to explore great themes such as the existence and nature of God, suffering, meaning and purpose.

Modern lives

St Paul described members of the Corinthian Church as '*a letter from Christ ... written not with ink but with the Spirit of the living God*' (2 Corinthians 3:3). In the first letter of St Peter, believers are described as 'living stones' who together make up a 'spiritual house' (1 Peter 2:5).

Important as buildings, works of art and literature are, the greatest heritage bequeathed to us by the Christian centuries are people whose lives have been touched by Christ. It is *people* who believe in, or deny or ignore, the Christian faith. It is *people* who encourage and inspire us to follow Christ – or who put us off.

I think it was the Jewish writer Martin Buber who suggested that, concerning belief in God, '*there are no evidences, only witnesses*'.

Eileen is a teacher from England who was forced to take early retirement because she suffers from multiple sclerosis. She continues to lead an active life although her mobility is severely limited. Two particular interests are music and enlisting support for *Save the Children* – which she does very effectively.

Eileen has a quiet faith. She does not feel angry at God for 'allowing' this to happen to her. She recognizes that illness and accidents are facts of life. Instead of asking, 'Why me?' she asks, 'Why not me?' She realizes that suffering is a problem which makes belief in God difficult for some people – but not for her. Eileen feels supported by friendship and by prayer. She retains her sense of humour and her peace of mind, as the following extract from one of her letters makes clear:

> *I've had to give up driving. The fatigue is rotten, but not such a worry now that I've stopped working. The blurred and double/triple vision is a nuisance, but curiously interesting – for example the Cathedral has had two spires for a couple of years, there are three moons in the sky and an awful lot of eight-legged cats about! I am quite used to it now and it's not a worry. I've made no retirement plans, confident that something will emerge for me, when the time is right.*

Following the Christian Way involves much more than 'going to church' or belonging to a cultural group. When it is true to itself, Christian faith engages with real life. It brings challenge and inspiration; it gives strength and comfort in trouble.

Being a Christian means ... being a person in whom his (Jesus') life and character and power are manifest and energized ... Christian experience is not so much a matter of imitating a leader as accepting and receiving a new quality of life – a life infinitely more profound and dynamic and meaningful than human life without Christ.

(Harry Williams CR, Anglican monk)
